"Entrepreneurship provides a blank canvas for Christians to put their belief into action, and in *Called to Create* Jordan gives us a strong theology and a great imagination for what this might look like in the world. This is key reading for both the aspiring entrepreneur and the active founder alike."

Dave Blanchard, CEO and cofounder of Praxis

"Creativity isn't optional, not if we're serious about conforming to the image of Christ. Creativity is the natural and supernatural byproduct of a Spirit-fill-d life. I'm so thankful Jordan wrote this book to challenge creativity and entrepreneurship as a n and loving others!"

Mark Batterson, *New York T. The Circle Maker* and lead pastor of National Community Church

"Creating a purpose-driven business or a nonprofit can be one of the significant ways to live out the gospel and serve others around you. This book will inspire and challenge you to action and change."

Scott Harrison, founder and CEO of Charity: Water

"I have had the privilege of starting several businesses, both secular and faith-based, but have never written about my experiences. I would hope that, had I done so, my book would have been the one that Jordan Raynor has written. He has captured the essence of being entrepreneurial and—better yet—being an entrepreneur following the call of God. At my age and stage of life I am looking back with fulfillment and gratitude that when God calls, he also equips. May thousands of new entrepreneurs read this book and follows God's call to create for the glory of the Great Creator."

Ron Blue, founding director of Kingdom Advisors

"Millions of Jesus followers live in suspended animation, missing their true destiny in Christ and vocation. *Called to Create* is a tomahawk missile on course to set these captives free and invite them into a wild adventure of honoring God in the marketplace, reimagining calling, purpose, and vocation while embracing whole-life discipleship. It is a bold work that will inevitably change lives . . . perhaps yours!"

Mike Sharrow, president and CEO of The C12 Group

"*Called to Create* is a book that will warm your soul and light a fire in your heart. In this book, Jordan has brought to light an aspect of God's character that is both beautiful and compelling. His words will inspire you to look at your creative work—whatever it may be—as an act of worship and a reflection of God himself. *Called to Create* gives validation to the creative work you do and challenges you to continue that work as a service to the world around you. You will be motivated to go create something beautiful and live out the calling on your heart. *Called to Create* is the book that will give you the confidence to say, 'My work is valuable.' This is a must-read book for all Christian creatives, whether you've started your work or are still dreaming about it."

Krystal Whitten, creator of The Lettering Prayer Journal

"Whether you're a business owner, an entrepreneurial employee, a student looking to make something of the world, the founder of a nonprofit, a mompreneur, a photographer, a painter, a musician, an author, or a chef, *Called to Create* will help you see how your creative work can be an act of worship to God. There is no hierarchy of callings, whereby 'ministers' or 'missionaries' are the only ones doing the work of the Lord. God has called us all, and in *Called to Create*, Jordan debunks this bad theology and offers Christian creators an inspiring, biblically based invitation to embrace creativity as a means of serving God and others."

Mark Russell, PhD, founder of Elevate Publishing
and author of *Our Souls at Work*, *Work as Worship*,
and *The Missional Entrepreneur*

called to

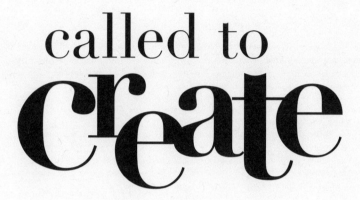

called to create

A Biblical Invitation to Create, Innovate, and Risk

jordan raynor

BakerBooks

a division of Baker Publishing Group
Grand Rapids, Michigan

Published by Baker Books
a division of Baker Publishing Group
P.O. Box 6287, Grand Rapids, MI 49516-6287
www.bakerbooks.com

Printed in the United States of America

Library of Congress Cataloging-in-Publication Data
Names: Raynor, Jordan, 1986– author.
Title: Called to create : a biblical invitation to create, innovate, and risk / Jordan Raynor.
Description: Grand Rapids : Baker Books, 2017. | Includes bibliographical references.
Identifiers: LCCN 2017020774 | ISBN 9780801075186 (pbk.)
Subjects: LCSH: Creative ability—Religious aspects—Christianity. | Creation (Literary, artistic, etc.)—Religious aspects—Christianity. | Vocation—Christianity.
Classification: LCC BT709.5 .R39 2017 | DDC 248.8/8—dc23
LC record available at https://lccn.loc.gov/2017020774

17 18 19 20 21 22 23   8 7 6 5 4 3

For the One
who has called me
to create

contents

Introduction   11

part 1: calling

1. The First Entrepreneur   23

2. The Goodness of Work   37

3. Discerning Our Calling   51

part 2: creating

4. Why We Create   69

5. What We Create   83

6. How We Create   99

part 3: challenges

7. Trust, Hustle, and Rest   119

8. Responding to Failure   135

9. Renewing Our Minds   151

part 4: charge

10. Commanded to Create Disciples 169
11. The Purpose of Profit 189
12. Creating for the Kingdom 205

Acknowledgments 219
About the Author 223
Notes 225

introduction

God was the first entrepreneur. He brought something out of nothing. He established order out of chaos. He created for the good of others. Before the Bible tells us that God is loving, holy, or merciful, we learn that he is creative.

We are made in the image of the First Entrepreneur; thus, when we follow his call to create businesses, nonprofits, art, music, books, and other products, we are not just doing something good for the world, we are doing something God-like. This is important because it validates the deep desire in our souls to create.

If you've ever felt like your work as a Christian entrepreneur or creative is anything less than God-like service to the world, this book is for you. If you've ever wanted your work to feel like a calling rather than a job, this book is for you. If you've ever wanted to sit down with dozens of Christian creators to better understand how they connect their faith to their work, this book is most certainly for you.

This book started out with a set of questions I've accumulated through years of seeking to more deeply integrate my Christian faith with my work as an entrepreneur and creative. Rather than answering all of these questions myself, I have spent almost two years posing them to dozens of Christian entrepreneurs through first-person interviews and research. The stories of these men and women are what make up the majority of this book.

Blake Mycoskie, the founder of TOMS Shoes, helps us understand how we can do ministry without abandoning a passion for entrepreneurship. Krystal Whitten, the creator of the *Lettering Prayer Journal*, puts a face to the deep guilt many moms face for following both the call to create and the call to motherhood. C. S. Lewis, Arthur Guinness, and Scott Harrison of Charity: Water show us how we can create products that reveal God's character and love others. The founders of In-N-Out Burger, Chick-fil-A, and Sevenly demonstrate how the gospel can influence every aspect of how we run our ventures. Nicole Baker Fulgham, founder of the nonprofit The Expectations Project, shows us how to manage the tension between trusting in God and hustling to grow our organizations. Hymnwriter and entrepreneur Horatio Spafford provides an inspiring case study for how creators should respond to inevitable adversity and failure. J. R. R. Tolkien and "the Inklings" model how Christian community can help renew our minds as we create. HTC cofounder Cher Wang demonstrates the multifaceted purpose of profit, while PayPal cofounder Peter Thiel casts a vision of heaven that gives deep meaning to our creating both today and for eternity. These are just some of the stories you will find in the following pages.[1]

Who Is an Entrepreneur?

Our collective fascination with the topic of entrepreneurship has risen drastically over the last century. The number of mentions of the word *entrepreneurship* in American books has increased sharply just in the last decade.[2] It's a word we throw around a lot. But it can be a difficult word to define. What exactly is entrepreneurship and who is an entrepreneur?

The word *entrepreneur* first appeared in a French dictionary in 1723 to describe a person who undertakes a task with financial risk.[3] Contemporary dictionaries define an entrepreneur similarly. Dictionary.com says an entrepreneur is "a person who organizes and manages any enterprise, especially a business, usually with considerable initiative and risk."[4] Merriam-Webster defines an entrepreneur as "one who organizes, manages, and assumes the risks of a business or enterprise."[5]

While these definitions are good, they leave something to be desired—namely the act of creating something new that many people associate with the work of entrepreneurs. Today when we hear the word *entrepreneur* people like Steve Jobs, Oprah Winfrey, and Mark Zuckerberg are among the first that come to mind. While it's true that these individuals "organized and managed" their enterprises at "considerable initiative and risk," these qualities alone didn't make them great entrepreneurs. We define these people as entrepreneurs because they created something new. They brought something out of relatively nothing. They established order out of chaos. And, through their creations, they loved and served the world.

So allow me to submit a new definition for the word *entrepreneur* to guide the rest of these pages: an entrepreneur is anyone who takes a risk to create something new for the good of others.

With this definition, Jobs, Winfrey, Zuckerberg, and others who traditionally identify as entrepreneurs obviously fit the bill. But it's not just these most obvious candidates whom this definition qualifies as entrepreneurs. This definition includes creators across the widest array of fame, fortune, geography, job title, company size, and industry. It includes entrepreneurial employees, nonprofit founders, mompreneurs, students looking to make something of the world, small business owners, and a growing number of self-identified creatives: photographers, painters, musicians, authors, Etsy shop owners, designers, architects, and chefs, all of whom risk financial and social capital to create something new for the good of others.

> An entrepreneur is anyone who takes a risk to create something new for the good of others.

As someone who fits the traditional definitions of both an "entrepreneur" and "creative," to me there's always been a clear connection between entrepreneurship and creativity. From my perspective, the act of creating a new business is not dissimilar to composing a song. Both require bringing something out of nothing, establishing order out of chaos, and creating something good for others. I think Steve Jobs understood this connection deeply. Arguably the most visionary and successful entrepreneur of the twentieth century, Jobs loved music. Eventually this manifested itself in the launch of the iPod, but long before that, Jobs was connecting music with his work as a tech entrepreneur. In 1988, Jobs was set to launch his highly anticipated NeXT Computer. Famous for obsessing over every detail of every product launch, it's notable that Jobs chose the Louise M. Davies Symphony Hall in San Francisco as the venue to launch his newest machine. In Aaron Sorkin's biopic film on Jobs, he portrays a heated conversation between Jobs and his Apple cofounder, Steve Wozniak. Standing among rows of music stands in the orchestra pit of Symphony Hall, Wozniak says to Jobs, "You can't write code. You're not an engineer. You're not a designer. So how come ten times in a day, I read Steve Jobs is a genius? *What* do you do?" Jobs replies, "I play the orchestra."[6] To explain his work as an entrepreneur, Jobs used a musical metaphor. Whether you identify as an entrepreneur or a creative, this book is for you. To Jobs and to me, the labels are essentially one and the same.

My Story

I haven't always thought of myself as an entrepreneur, but looking back over the course of my short life (I'm thirty as I write this), that label is probably the best way to describe my lifelong desire to create. I started my first "business" when I was nine years old, selling baseball cards out of my bedroom. It was a terrible business, as my customer acquisition strategy was totally reliant on the hospitality of my parents. In the eighth grade, my entrepreneurial spirit took a different shape as I watched the 2000 election, mesmerized by the romanticism that characterizes the startup-like launch, rise, and fall of presidential campaigns. That election started me down a political career path. At the age of seventeen, I took my first "real job" managing a campaign in my hometown of Tampa, Florida. After winning that election, I thought I was addicted to politics; but after more political jobs in college and an incredible experience working at the White House, I realized it wasn't politics and campaigns I loved. It was creating something out of nothing and winning. It was entrepreneurship.

As I was graduating from Florida State University in the spring of 2008, I had two job offers on the table: one to work for John McCain's presidential campaign and one to lead a growing political tech startup. The choice was an easy one. I took the entrepreneurial path and I never looked back. After leading somebody else's business for a year and a half, I decided it was time to launch my own—a digital marketing agency that serviced political campaigns, causes, and corporations. In 2011, my company was acquired by a "mega interactive agency" out of Washington, DC. After staying at the acquiring company for a little more than a year, I was ready to start up again. In 2012, my cofounders and I launched Citizinvestor, which today is the largest provider of crowdfunding software for municipalities in the United States.

It was during the building of Citizinvestor that I began seriously questioning my calling and whether or not I was serving the Lord through what I saw at the time as "secular" work. I grew up in the church and attended a Christian school where it seemed like every pastor and chapel speaker implied that if I *really* loved the Lord, if I was *really* sold out for Christ, I would go into "full-time ministry" or live in a mud hut three thousand miles away from home. At the same time, I grew up watching my father and grandfather live out their faith through their work as entrepreneurs. I was conflicted, to say the least. In the summer of 2014, I began to transition out of the day-to-day operations of Citizinvestor, and as you will read more about later in this book, I wasn't sure where God was calling me for the next chapter in my career.

On the one hand, it was clear to me that God had given me a passion for entrepreneurship, the giftings to be good at the craft, and clear opportunities to exercise those gifts to love others. On the other hand, I wondered whether it would be a more God-honoring, eternally significant use of my time to put those passions and skills to work in a more overtly evangelical context such as planting a church. Through much prayer, study of God's Word, and communion with other believers, I decided to continue down the path the Lord had already set me on and follow the call to create. In 2014, I launched a new company to help other entrepreneurs launch and grow their businesses. I named the company Vocreo, combining the Latin words *vocātiō* and *creo* to mean "called to create." In 2016, I took an indefinite leave of absence from the firm to take on the role of CEO at one of Vocreo's fastest growing portfolio companies: a venture-backed technology startup called Threshold 360.

What to Expect from This Book

This book is the result of nearly two years of research and dozens of conversations with other Christian entrepreneurs as I sought to answer some of my (and hopefully your) questions about what it means to be called to create, such as:

- How does God's creative and entrepreneurial character empower me to emulate Him?
- Is my work as an entrepreneur and creative really as God-honoring as that of a pastor or "full-time missionary"?
- What are the right questions to ask when discerning where God has called me to work?

- What does it look like to create not in order to make a name for myself but to glorify the One who has called me to create and love others?
- How does recognizing my work as a calling from God change my motivations for creating, what I create, and how I create it?
- What are the challenges unique to or especially acute for those who are called to create, and what's the proper way to deal with them?
- What is the purpose of profit?
- How can I use my work as an entrepreneur to fulfill Jesus's command to create disciples?
- While my work may matter today, will my creations live on into eternity?

With this book, I have taken a "show" rather than "tell" approach to answering these questions, bringing in colorful stories from more than forty men and women who have followed God's call to create. This is not a how-to book. This is a compilation of compelling stories that paint a picture of what it means to be called to create.

The book is organized into four parts. Part 1 deals with the issue of "calling," a loaded and often confusing term in the church today. In this part, we will take a deeper look at God's creative character, explore what the Bible has to say about the inherent goodness of work, and set forth a series of practical questions to help us discern our calling.

In part 2, we will examine how following the call to create impacts our motivations for creating, the products we choose to create, and what it looks like to holistically integrate the gospel into our ventures, beginning with striving for excellence in everything we do and prioritizing people over profit. As we'll see, our work can only be a calling if someone calls us to it and we work for their sake and not our own.

Part 3 deals with the challenges that are unique to or especially acute for the Christian entrepreneur, including managing the tension between trusting in God and hustling to make things happen in our ventures, responding to adversity and failure, and how we as Christians need to continually renew our minds through regular communion with God, our partners, and other believers.

> Our work can only be a calling if someone calls us to it and we work for their sake and not our own.

In part 4, we will issue a charge for those who are called to create, asking questions about what it looks like to create disciples through our endeavors, how we should view profit, and how what we create today can last on into eternity, as we lay our creations down at the feet of the First Entrepreneur as he builds his final masterpiece, the new heaven and new earth.

As you read through this book, you will undoubtedly want to take some time to think through the principles of each chapter and how they apply to your own endeavors. To facilitate this, I have developed a free *Called to Create* study journal with thought-provoking questions to accompany each chapter and plenty of space for you to take notes. To download this free study journal, visit calledtocreate.org/journal.

Now, are you ready to hear the stories of dozens of Christian entrepreneurs and creatives? Are you ready to embrace God's call to create in your life? Are you ready to think deeper about what it means to reimagine your creating as service to the One who has called you to create? Let's begin.

PART 1

calling

1

the first entrepreneur

Have you ever heard a sermon so compelling that you drove sixteen hours to thank the pastor in person for how their words changed your life? Kristin Joy Taylor has. In 2008, Jerry King, a pastor from Mansfield, Ohio, was guest preaching at Taylor's home church in Tampa, Florida. From the pulpit he shared:

> God presents himself in the Bible first of all as the Creator God. He could have begun this story in lots of different ways, but the place he chose to say "Human beings, this is who I am, I want you to know *this* about me first," is here: I am the Creator God. And so the very first chapters of Genesis begin with these unfolding stories of God in action creating out of nothing, bringing into being, stage by stage, day by day, everything that is. If you are one who has a greater amount of creativity in you, you have a place at the table of God's people and of humanity. You're valid. Step up. Bring what you've got. Don't you dare hold back. Not cringing back, not with arrogant pride, with sane humility bring your stuff. Other people need it.[1]

Those words brought a leap to Kristin Joy Taylor's spirit and tears to her eyes. An entrepreneur, painter, and photographer, Taylor had always been creative, but until hearing that sermon, she had never understood that when she created, she was emulating her Creator. "All my life, I always knew I was creative, but there was no validity for my creative work being a calling from God. Creativity was kind of always on the fringes," she said. "That sermon gave me a huge validation in my spirit that creativity is not a fringe thing but is central and of infinite worth, because we are made in the image of God."

Days after the sermon, Taylor was sharing how impactful these truths were with a friend who was equally moved by Pastor King's words. The two women decided that, just as King had validated them, they needed to validate him and his ministry. So they asked their congregation to write letters to King, sharing the impact his words had on their lives. With the letters in hand, they hopped into Taylor's Honda Civic and drove sixteen hours from Tampa, Florida, to Mansfield, Ohio, to deliver the thank-you letters in person.

Why did this sermon stir up such a radical response from these two women? I think it's because that in the church we often hear that God is loving, holy, omnipotent, sovereign, just, merciful, and faithful. But we rarely, if ever, hear that God is entrepreneurial. Yet, as King pointed out, that is the first characteristic revealed about God in the Bible!

"In the beginning God created the heavens and the earth. Now the earth was formless and empty, darkness was over the surface of the deep, and the Spirit of God was hovering over the waters. And God said, 'Let there be light,' and there was light" (Gen. 1:1–3). If you're like me, you have read this passage so many times that it can be easy to miss the magnitude of what's happening here. In the beginning, "the earth was formless and empty" (v. 2). It wasn't until God took action that this formless void began to be filled. God brought something out of nothing. He brought order out of chaos. God was the first entrepreneur.

> God brought something out of nothing. He brought order out of chaos. God was the first entrepreneur.

The First Entrepreneur

As we established in the introduction, an entrepreneur is anyone who takes a risk to create something new for the good of others. With this definition, the Creator of the universe certainly qualifies as the first entrepreneur. In Genesis, God is clearly creating something new. In six days, he created the heavens, the earth, light, evening, morning, sky, land, sea, vegetation, sun, moon, stars, animals, and human beings. All of this was thoroughly original, as the earth was "formless and empty" prior to God speaking these things into existence. C. S. Lewis gives us a picture of this in *The Magician's Nephew*, giving readers a front-row seat to Aslan (the God-like lion) singing the land of Narnia into existence. As the characters step into what is about to become Narnia, one of them remarks that, "This is an empty world. This is Nothing." Lewis continues:

> And really it was uncommonly like Nothing. There were no stars. It was so dark that they couldn't see one another at all and it made no difference whether you kept your eyes shut or open. Then . . . the blackness overhead, all at once, was

blazing with stars. They didn't come out gently one by one, as they do on a summer evening. One moment there had been nothing but darkness; next moment a thousand, thousand points of light leaped out—single stars, constellations, and planets, brighter and bigger than any in our world.²

Not only did God create something new but, equally important for our definition of entrepreneurship, he created something for the good of others. Have you ever wondered why God created the world and humankind? He certainly didn't need to. So, in one sense, God appears to have created for the pure joy of doing it. As you read through Genesis 1, you can't help but imagine God having a ball bringing everything into being, flinging the stars into the sky and turning the oceans loose. God created because he wanted to. But *why* did he want to? The great theologian Jonathan Edwards once said, "What God aimed at in the creation of the world, as the end which he had ultimately in view, was that communication of himself which he intended through all eternity."³ If God is the source of all goodness, then revealing himself and his character to us is one of the most loving things he could do. So God appears to have created for the good of others by revealing his character, but Genesis hints at a second way in which the First Entrepreneur loved others through his creating. In Genesis 1:26 we find the word "our" for the first time in Scripture, indicating that the God of the Bible is a triune God, comprised of Father, Son, and Holy Spirit. Before God brought the world into being, the Trinity had been enjoying perfect community, submitting to each other, loving each other, and serving each other for all eternity. Jesus's prayer prior to his crucifixion gives us beautiful insight into the Trinity's relationship:

> [Jesus] looked toward heaven and prayed: "Father, the hour has come. Glorify your Son, that your Son may glorify you. For you granted him authority over all people that he might give eternal life to all those you have given him. Now this is eternal life: that they know you, the only true God, and Jesus Christ, whom you have sent. I have brought you glory on earth by finishing the work you gave me to do. And now, Father, glorify me in your presence with the glory I had with you before the world began. (John 17:1–5)

The Trinity shows us the others-orientation of the Godhead. God is selfless, constantly submitting to each of the other members of the Trinity. So it stands to reason that one of the primary reasons why God created was to share the perfect love the Trinity has been experiencing for all eternity with us. His creating was a way of serving us, by making us in his image so we could experience a glimpse of the joy he has been experiencing for all of time.

Finally, while God clearly created something new for the good of others, did omnipotent God really take a risk when he created? As pastor Timothy Keller[4] shared with a group of Christian entrepreneurs:

> You can see the risks and the costs from the very beginning. God made the world filled with human beings made in His image, human beings with freewill. So God made the world knowing what it was going to cost Him. Knowing what we were going to do. Knowing that [His] Son was going to have to come into the world and experience what he experienced.[5]

One of the most defining characteristics of entrepreneurship is risk. When we fashion creation in a fresh new way to bring about something new, there is a tremendous amount of uncertainty. We are not omniscient and thus do not know whether our creations will fail or succeed. But God *is* omniscient. He *is* all-knowing. When God created humankind, he knew precisely the risks he was taking and yet still created out of a desire to share his love with us.

There's one other difference between God's creating and ours that's worth noting before we move on. In Genesis 1:1, when it tells us for the first time that God "created," the Hebrew word used in the original manuscripts is *bara*, meaning "to create," connoting the idea of creating something out of nothing. When God begins to take action in the creation account, "the earth was formless and empty," giving God nothing to create with. While the song "Beautiful Things" is correct in saying that God "makes beautiful things out of the dust," God is also the only One who makes beautiful things out of absolutely nothing.[6] This is different from the way human beings create, rearranging raw materials and resources (money, time, physical goods, etc.) to bring about something new. But as Andy Crouch, executive editor of *Christianity Today* and author of *Culture Making*,[7] points out:

> The difference is not as great as you might think. For every act of creation involves bringing something into being that was not there before—every creation is *ex nihilo*, from nothing, even when it takes the world as its starting point. Something is added in every act of making. This is clearest in the realm of art, where the raw materials of pigment and canvas become more than you ever could have predicted. Even a five-year-old's finger painting is more than the sum of paper and paint.

But creation, the marvelous making of more than was there before, also happens when a chef makes an omelet, when a carpenter makes a chair, when a toddler makes a snow angel.⁸

The creation account clearly reveals God as infinitely creative and entrepreneurial. But God doesn't just reveal these characteristics to us in Genesis. Throughout Scripture, God shows us his entrepreneurial character through each of the members of the Trinity: Father, Spirit, and Son.

The Spirit

In the book of the Bible immediately following Genesis, where we read the account of the First Entrepreneur's creation of the world, we meet a man named Bezalel, who is in need of being filled by the Spirit of God in order to build the Tabernacle, a dwelling place for God on earth. The writer of Exodus shares:

> Then the LORD said to Moses, "See, I have chosen Bezalel son of Uri, the son of Hur, of the tribe of Judah, and I have filled him with the Spirit of God, with wisdom, with understanding, with knowledge and with all kinds of skills—to make artistic designs for work in gold, silver and bronze, to cut and set stones, to work in wood, and to engage in all kinds of crafts." (Exod. 31:1–5)

Bezalel was an entrepreneur and artist who was being commissioned by God himself. But before Bezalel could begin the work of rearranging the raw materials of gold, silver, bronze, stone, and wood to create something new, God had to fill him with his Spirit. Why? Because God is the First Entrepreneur and the source of all creativity and ingenuity.

In order for Bezalel to create the Tabernacle of the Lord, he needed more of God's likeness.

To fully appreciate what is going on in this account in Exodus, we must note that the Tabernacle was a physical representation of "the universe the way it ought to be"[9] with God at the center of it. The design of the interior of the Tabernacle pointed worshipers to the Holy of Holies, an interior room in which the Israelites believed God physically existed. The Tabernacle was essentially its own world, with everything pointing toward God. So when God called Bezalel to create the Tabernacle, he was inviting him to mimic God's creation of earth, thus bringing glory to God by emulating his creative Spirit.

> God is the source of all creativity and ingenuity.

The Carpenter

Nearly fifteen hundred years after Bezalel used his God-given skills of craftsmanship to create a dwelling place for God, God himself came to earth as a human and spent 85 percent of his working life leveraging a skillset very similar to Bezalel's to run a small business.

The Bible gives us very little detail of Jesus's life between the ages of twelve and thirty, when he began his public ministry. One of the only things Scripture notes about this significant period of time is that he was known in his community for his work as a carpenter (Mark 6:3). This is remarkable! The only thing the Bible tells us about what Jesus was doing for half of his life was working. But Jesus wasn't doing just any work; he was doing the work of a creator and entrepreneur, revealing to us this important characteristic of his Father, and indeed, the Trinity.

While many Christians know that Jesus was a carpenter, our modern understanding of this vocation might not align with the work Jesus actually did. As biblical scholar Dr. Ken Campbell points out, the Greek term *tektōn* that most English Bibles translate as "carpenter" in Mark 6:3 would more accurately be translated as "builder," someone who "worked with stone, wood, and sometimes metal" to create something new for the good of others. Jesus, alongside his earthly father, Joseph, owned a family-operated small business, "negotiating bids, securing supplies, completing projects, and contributing to family living expenses." In first-century Jewish culture, it was artisans and craftspeople like Jesus who "had the ancient equivalent of small, independent businesses" and would be called entrepreneurs by us today.[10]

From the beginning of time, God knew that Jesus would be sent to earth to be raised by Mary and Joseph, a creator and entrepreneur. Given the trajectory of Jesus's life and his ultimate purpose for coming to earth, this fact should give us great pause. Dr. Klaus Issler, a professor of theology at Biola University, ponders this, saying:

> It might have been important for the Messiah—like the prophet Samuel and John the Baptist—to grow up in a priestly household. He could have devoted days to prayer and the study of Scripture as well as had daily access to the temple precincts. Or, perhaps the Messiah could have been raised within a Pharisee's household as was true for the Apostle Paul.[11]

But God didn't choose to place Jesus in a priestly or Pharisaical household. Jesus was placed in the home of small

31

business owners, where for twenty years he would reveal God's character (*his* character) as an entrepreneur, creating new things for the good of others.

Throughout the New Testament, Jesus speaks of his desire to glorify God the Father. *Glorify* is one of those church words that is thrown around so much its meaning is often muddled. As pastor John Piper says, to glorify God simply means to "reflect his greatness" or reveal his characteristics to others.[12] Thus, one of the primary reasons God chose to humble himself and come to earth as a human being was so that Jesus could reveal God's character through human speech and mannerisms that we could more easily understand. In just three years of public ministry, Jesus revealed countless characteristics about his Father. To the woman at the well, Jesus showed us that God is omniscient. To the five thousand, Jesus showed us that God is our provider.

> The fact that Jesus spent twenty years as a carpenter revealing God's creative and entrepreneurial spirit should stop us in our tracks.

To Lazarus, Jesus showed us that God is the giver of life. And on the cross, Jesus showed us that "God so loved the world" that he would sacrifice his only Son in order to spend eternity with us. If Jesus was able to reveal so much of God's character in such a relatively short period of time, the fact that Jesus spent twenty years revealing God's creative and entrepreneurial spirit should stop us in our tracks.

Even Jesus's death and resurrection reveal the creative character of God. In 2 Corinthians 5:17 we are told that "if anyone is in Christ, he is a new creature; the old things passed away; behold, new things have come" (NASB). It is at the cross that we see God's final entrepreneurial endeavor on this side of eternity. The investment God made at the beginning of time to create a world for us came with ultimate risk. On the cross, that risk was fully realized, but the dividends were obviously worth the cost. Through our trust in Jesus's sacrifice as the sole atonement for our sins, God has made us a new creation, righteous in his eyes, able to spend eternity with him.

Co-creators

For my daughter's first Christmas, my wife and I bought her a miniature baby grand piano.[13] On Christmas morning, we wrapped it in a big red bow and set it between the Christmas tree and my full-size baby grand. When we sat my daughter down at her piano for the first time, she banged the keys as hard as she could, setting off a cacophony of sound while flashing the biggest smile a toothless four-month-old can muster. Her joy instantly became our joy. This joy had two dimensions. First, as with any of the thousand "firsts" a child experiences in their first year of life, I was overjoyed to see my daughter experience Christmas and play her own piano for the first time. But because of my personal love for music and the significant role the piano has played in my life, there was a second dimension to my joy. While watching my daughter tinker with the keys of her piano, I saw myself in her. She was unknowingly reflecting a small part of my character and personality for the first time. The joy I felt in that moment must be just a fraction of the joy God experiences when he sees his character reflected in his children.

As we've seen, throughout time God has revealed himself as a creator and entrepreneur. And as we pick back up in Genesis, we find God calling us to be co-creators with him so that we might bring him joy by reflecting his character.

What God created in six days is astonishing. But what's equally remarkable is what he did *not* create. He created animals but he didn't give them names. He created land but he didn't create irrigation systems. He created stars but he didn't create an iPhone app that would allow us to hold a pocket-sized computer up to the sky to see them all by name. After working for six days, God left the earth largely undeveloped and uncultivated. He created a canvas and then invited us to join him in filling it. Let's pick up in Genesis 1 with God's final creation on the sixth day: "God created man in His own image, in the image of God He created him; male and female He created them" (Gen. 1:27 NASB). The dominant characteristic God has revealed about himself up until this point in Scripture is that he is a Creator. So when human beings are created "in His own image" the logical implication is that they will be characterized by the creativity of their Creator. As Piper says:

> When the first chapter of the Bible says, "God created man in his own image, in the image of God he created him; male and female he created them" (Gen. 1:27), what is the point? The point of an image is to image. Images are erected to display the original. Point to the original. Glorify the original. God made humans in his image so that the world would be filled with reflectors of God. Images of God. Seven billion statues of God. So that nobody would miss the point of creation. Nobody (unless they were stone blind) could miss the point of humanity, namely, God. Knowing, loving, showing God.[14]

34

But just in case we miss God's intention that we emulate his creative character, he uses his first words to humankind to issue a job description, an explicit call to create:

God blessed them and said to them, "Be fruitful and increase in number; fill the earth and subdue it. Rule over the fish in the sea and the birds in the sky and over every living creature that moves on the ground." Then God said, "I give you every seed-bearing plant on the face of the whole earth and every tree that has fruit with seed in it. They will be yours for food. And to all the beasts of the earth and all the birds in the sky and all the creatures that move along the ground—everything that has the breath of life in it—I give every green plant for food." And it was so. God saw all that he had made, and it was very good. And there was evening, and there was morning—the sixth day (vv. 28–31).

Before the First Entrepreneur takes a day of rest, he puts a succession plan in place by creating man and woman in his image and calling them to create. At first glance, the command in this passage may appear to simply be a call to reproduce, but as Keller points out, the call is much more than that:

First, we are called to "fill the earth"—to increase in number. While God usually says of plants and animals "let them" multiply (Gen. 11, 20a, 20b, 22, and 24), human beings are not only given a command to do so actively (v. 28a) but then receive a detailed job description (vv. 28b–29). In other words, only humans are given multiplication as a task to fulfill with intention. But why would this be a job—isn't it just a natural process? Not exactly. Human beings "filling the earth" means something far [more] than plants and animals filling

35

the earth. It means civilization, not just procreation. We get the sense that God does not want merely more individuals of the human species; he also wants the world to be filled with a human society.[15]

God created us to be co-creators with him, to do "the things that God has done in creation—bringing order out of chaos" to create new things for the good of others. God is calling us to be entrepreneurial.[16] Fuller Seminary president Richard Mouw put it this way:

> God created us to be co-creators with him. God is calling us to be entrepreneurial.

> God is an entrepreneur. He leveraged His resources at great cost to Himself. He made space in the universe for us. So, if you see a human need not being met, you see a talent that can meet that need, if you invest your resources so that the talent can meet that need, and you create new value in the world, new goods to be shared, better quality of life, or human community flourishing, then what you've done is not just godly, but God-like.[17]

As we've seen, God went to great lengths to demonstrate his creative and entrepreneurial character through his Word. But while Scripture clearly treats emulating this character as "godly" and "God-like," the church often explicitly and implicitly views the work of creators as "secular" and less spiritual than the work of the pastor or "full-time missionary." Why? That's the question we turn to next.

2

the goodness of work

Knowing what we now know about God's character and how we are made in his creative image, we might think that Christians would be known as especially creative and entrepreneurial. But as Andy Crouch points out, that's not the case:

> I wonder what we Christians are known for in the world outside our churches. Are we known as critics, consumers, copiers, condemners of culture? I'm afraid so. Why aren't we known as cultivators—people who tend and nourish what is best in human culture, who do the hard and painstaking work to preserve the best of what people before us have done? Why aren't we known as creators—people who dare to think and do something that has never been thought or done before, something that makes the world more welcoming and thrilling and beautiful?[1]

The thrust of Crouch's questions is this: Knowing what we know of God's creative character, why don't more Christians feel called to emulate their Creator? The idea that the work of entrepreneurs is a "calling" from God is counterintuitive for many. But it's not just creative and entrepreneurial work that Christians don't feel called to but "secular" work in general. A 2013 study by the Barna Group found that only one-third of American Christians "feel called to the work they currently do."[2] With Americans working an average of forty-seven hours per week, this means that American Christians spend roughly 40 percent of their waking hours doing work that they see little to no eternal meaning in.[3] How depressing!

Over the course of my career, I have thought a lot about this issue and discussed this topic at length with friends inside and outside of the world of entrepreneurship. It seems clear to me that the church has bought into a false storyline about work that says work is inherently bad and meaningless unless it is "full-time ministry." Before we discern the calling of entrepreneurs specifically, we must first combat this thinking with biblical truths that give us a much more hopeful and meaningful storyline for all work.

Work Is Inherently Good

Before you read the previous chapter of this book, what images would have come to mind if I asked you to picture Adam and Eve in the Garden of Eden? You may have envisioned a beautiful garden, luscious fruits and vegetables, perfect animals, and a crystal-clear stream of water. But would you have seen Adam and Eve working? Because of the false storyline many have bought about work, that's probably not the first image that would have come to your mind. But the Genesis account reminds us that work was a central part of life for Adam and Eve in perfect Eden and thus is not at all inherently bad. In fact, Genesis 2:15 shows us that God intends work to be an act of worship! As my pastor, Chris Basham, points out:

> In Genesis 2:15, we are told that, "God took the man and put him in the Garden of Eden to work it and take care of it." The Hebrew word translated as "put" (*wayyannihehu*) in this verse does not simply mean to place an object. The word connotes rest and safety as well as dedication in God's presence. God specifically put man in the garden where he could be safe and rest, and where he could have fellowship with God. Mankind's primary responsibility there was to worship and obey God. Adam served—and thereby worshipped God—through his work. Work is a good gift from God, not a punishment for sin.[4]

It's interesting that it was not until God put humankind to work that he was able to step back and say that his creation was "*very* good" and rest. Even God's resting points to the inherent goodness of work. Clearly, all-powerful God did not need to rest after bringing all things into existence. But he did. Why? I don't think it's farfetched to conclude that because God created work as a form of worship, he knew we would be tempted to work nonstop without taking time to rest and simply enjoy God, his people, and the fruits of our labor. It seems to me that God rested because he knew we might forget to.

At the opposite bookend of time, the Bible teaches us that work will also be a central component of life in heaven. In Revelation 22:3, we are told that "[God's] servants will serve him" in heaven. Service is something that is active, not passive. It involves expending energy and getting things done. Contrary to the caricature of heaven being a glorified retirement home, the Bible teaches that we will continue to work for eternity, serving God with our unique gifts (more to come on this in chapter 12). Victor Hugo, the author of masterpieces such as *Les Misérables* and *The Hunchback of Notre-Dame*, captured this idea of eternal work beautifully:

> I feel within me the future life. I shall most certainly rise toward the heavens. The nearer my approach to the end, the plainer is the sound of immortal symphonies of worlds which invite me. For half a century I have been writing my thoughts in prose and in verse; history, philosophy, drama, romance, tradition, satire, ode, and song; all of these have I tried. But I feel that I haven't given utterance to the thousandth part of what lies within me. When I go to the grave I can say as others have said, "I have finished my day's work." But I cannot say, "I have finished my life." My day's work will begin again the next morning. The tomb is not a blind alley; it is a thoroughfare. It closes on the twilight, but opens on the dawn.[5]

> While work can be arduous today, it is not inherently bad. It is so good that we will work for the glory of God forever.

The work Hugo (and we) anticipate in the next life, and the work Adam and Eve began in Eden, is similar to but at the same time starkly different from the work we do today. When sin entered the garden, work became difficult, exhausting, and frustrating, as we all experience today. But the Bible reminds us that, while work can be arduous today, it is not inherently bad. It is so good that we will work for the glory of God forever.

Work Is Meaningful

On March 24, 2005, more than eleven million people tuned their TVs to NBC to watch the US premiere of *The Office*, a comedy about the mundane and seemingly meaningless work of the employees of Dunder Mifflin, a dying regional paper and office supply distributor.[6] What came next was nothing short of a phenomenon as the show became an instant favorite of a generation of millennials coming of age at a time when jobs were few and many would be happy for any paycheck, even if they had to put up with a boss as incompetent and offensive as the show's Michael Scott. In retrospect, *The Office* seems to be a caricature of Americans' modern view of work: that work is a meaningless means to an end, a paycheck that allows us to enjoy the truly meaningful things in life.

But what if the employees of Dunder Mifflin knew and understood the truths we have just begun to explore in this book? What if they understood that because God calls us to work, all work has meaning and can be used to love and serve our neighbors? Then even the most mundane task of selling a pallet of paper has meaning because the Creator of the universe has ordained work so that we can help carry out his will on earth. What the Dunder Mifflin employees probably couldn't see was that the selling of that pallet of paper was used by God to carry out his will in countless ways. For the people who manufactured, sold, and distributed the paper, Dunder Mifflin provided income and thus put food on their families' tables and roofs over their heads. For the Dunder Mifflin employees, the profits from that pallet of paper allowed them to keep their jobs and continue working within a community of (mostly) loving friends. For all we know, the paper could have been delivered to a law firm who used the paper as a critical tool in fighting for justice in the world or securing families for orphans through adoption. All of these things matter to God, but he chooses to use our work to accomplish them. As Jeff Van Duzer puts it in *Why Business Matters to God*, "When businesses produce material things that enhance the welfare of the community, they are engaged in work that matters to God."[7]

If you think this example of a fictional paper distributor is small and contrived, look at the much more extreme, real-world story of Casper ten Boom, a devout Christian and thoroughly ordinary watchmaker who spent more than sixty years running the small business his father started in Haarlem, Netherlands, in 1837. From an outsider's perspective, ten Boom's work probably looked meaningless and mundane. For decades, he followed the same routines and patterns in operating his watch shop. But as his daughter Corrie remembers in her bestselling book *The Hiding Place*, ten Boom was a man who loved his work:

> For in addition to his twinkling eyes and long cigar-sweet beard, Father ticked. Watches lying on a shelf run differently from watches carried about, and so Father always wore the ones he was regulating. His suit jackets had four huge inside pockets, each fitted with hooks for a dozen watches, so that wherever he went the hum of hundreds of little wheels went gaily with him.[8]

Casper ten Boom lived and breathed his work. So much so that his watch shop was connected to the ten Booms' home ("the Beje") where he lived in tight quarters with his wife, adult daughters, and sisters-in-law. By all accounts, ten Boom loved his work. I believe this is because he understood that all work—even that of an ordinary watchmaker—has deep, eternal meaning.

Throughout ten Boom's life, God used the watch shop to accomplish his will. Like clockwork, every morning at 8:30 ten Boom would begin the day by leading his employees and family in Bible reading. In this way, he was a pastor of sorts, using his business to disciple and love his employees. But it wasn't just his staff he loved. The ten Boom family had a reputation for loving people and cultivating community. Located on the busy *Barteljorisstraat* that runs through the middle of Haarlem, the watch shop served as a community center of sorts, and ten Boom was the unofficial mayor, deemed "Haarlem's Grand Old Man" by the small town's residents.[9] While ten Boom was faithful in using his business to serve the Lord in "the little things," God had plans to entrust him with much more responsibility as Europe headed into World War II.

After the German occupation of Haarlem in 1940, the ten Boom family began leading a clandestine effort to hide Jews and others at risk of extermination by the Nazis. After successfully hiding a few Jews in the Beje, the ten Booms were soon confronted with another problem: providing food for their hidden guests. With the occupation, the Germans required Haarlem's residents to use food ration cards to feed themselves. These cards were not made available to Jews. Corrie ten Boom quickly found a fellow citizen who had the ability and willingness to smuggle these ration cards to the ten Boom residence. But transferring these ration cards in public was not an option. Corrie suggested that the man dress as an electric meterman, hiding the cards under his shirt and entering through the front door of the watch shop as if conducting a routine check on the shop's electrical meter. The ploy worked, and the watch shop quickly became the front door for the anti-Nazi underground network.

As the Nazis became more aggressive in their efforts to rid the world of God's people, the ten Booms used the watch shop in increasingly creative ways. As Corrie explained:

> Although we had a friend at the telephone exchange, we could never be sure that our line was not tapped. So we developed a system for coding our underground messages in terms of watches. "We have a woman's watch here that needs repairing. But I can't find a mainspring. Do you know who might have one?" (We have a Jewish woman in need of a hiding place and we can't find one among our regular contacts.) "I have a watch here with a face that's causing difficulty. One of the numbers has worked loose and it's holding back the hand. Do you know anyone who does this kind of repair work?" (We have a Jew here whose features are especially Semitic. Do you know anyone who would be willing to take an extra risk?) "I'm sorry, but the child's watch you left with us is not repairable. Do you have the receipt?" (A Jewish child has died in one of our houses. We need a burial permit.)[10]

On February 28, 1944, German soldiers raided the Beje, sending Casper, Corrie, and other members of their family to prison. At the time, the ten Booms were hiding four Jews and two members of the underground network in their home. When the ten Booms were taken away from the Beje, they didn't know if these six people were dead or alive, adding to their anguish. Weeks later, while in solitary confinement at Scheveningen concentration camp, Corrie received an encoded message informing her that "All the watches in your closet are safe." Corrie knew that the six had made it out alive.[11] But Casper ten Boom died only ten days after the raid, before he could hear the news that his watch shop had been used in this dramatic way to accomplish God's will one more time.

I recently had a chance to visit the watch shop, which is still operating in Haarlem. As I walked down the still-busy *Barteljorisstraat*, I was startled by how ordinary and unassuming the shop is.[12] Most people walked by without giving the shop a second look. I'm sure many of Haarlem's residents looked at Casper ten Boom's work as a watchmaker the same way, wondering what meaning there was in tinkering with timepieces for sixty years. But ten Boom leveraged his business in some incredibly meaningful ways. And while our stories will almost certainly not be as dramatic as ten Boom's, the fact is that all work is meaningful and can be used by God at any time, in any situation, to accomplish his will.

> All work is meaningful and can be used by God to accomplish his will.

All Callings Equal

Joel Ohman grew up in a conservative Christian home in America's heartland. After high school, he chose to attend Clearwater Christian College in Florida, partly because of his parents' encouragement to attend a Christian university and partly because he wanted to be close to the beach. Most recently, Ohman earned his master of divinity from Southeastern Baptist Theological Seminary.

Looking at this profile and the trajectory of his life, you might assume that Joel Ohman is preparing for a career as a pastor. But Ohman is a serial entrepreneur, the founder and CEO of a slew of impressive digital media companies including Exercise.com. As he shares, "Growing up in the church, there's a tendency to have a hierarchy of callings, to elevate the callings of the pastor or the missionary overseas. Whether they're explicitly saying it or not, they are pushing you in the direction of making 'full-time ministry' your career as well."

The idea that there is some "hierarchy of callings" has always bothered Ohman, as it seemed out of line with what the Bible teaches about work. While a student at Clearwater Christian College, he recalls sitting in the pew during a weekly chapel service, listening to a pastor "insinuate that if you're not planning on going into 'full-time ministry,' you aren't following God's calling for your life." After the sermon, Ohman approached the pastor and asked, "Are you telling me that if I believe God is calling me to be an entrepreneur, I should follow your advice and your personal calling instead?" The pastor then backtracked his statements.

> The metaphorical space between the "ordained" and the "ordinary" in the church is unfortunate and unbiblical.

Throughout his life, Ohman has studied God's Word and the truths outlined in this book, and said, "It is so freeing to realize that God has called me—with just as important a calling as that of any pastor—to create new things." A recent personality assessment confirmed for Ohman what he already knew. "The assessment showed me that I am skilled at casting vision and creating systems to bring those visions to life. That's creating new things. That's creating something out of nothing. That sounds arrogant apart from the fact that God has called us—has called *me*—to do just that."

Dr. Benjamin Quinn (who taught Ohman's Doctrine of Work course at Southeastern) writes in his book *Every Waking Hour* that:

> I [have been] awakened to the problem of the pulpit-pew divide—the centuries-old chasm between those who occupy the pulpit and those who occupy the pew. The physical space between pulpit and pew in worship spaces is necessary for practical reasons. The metaphorical space between the "ordained" and the "ordinary" in the church, however, is unfortunate and unbiblical.[13]

This pervasive idea that there is a hierarchy of callings for Christians is out of line with Scripture and much of church history. Martin Luther, John Calvin, and other leaders of the sixteenth-century Protestant Reformation argued that *all* work, even "secular" work, is as much a calling from God as the work of a pastor or priest.[14] In the words of DC Comics' artist Dave Gibbons, "The highest calling is not being a pastor but becoming all God called you to be, namely a person who glorifies God in all you do."[15]

> The highest calling is not being a pastor but becoming all God called you to be.

But it's not just professional callings that the church tends to assign hierarchy to. As Krystal Whitten, a wife, mother, Sunday school leader, and entrepreneur, reminded me, each of us has multiple callings, but when a Christian (*especially* a Christian woman) chooses to follow God's call to create, they are often told explicitly and implicitly that their professional calling is inferior to their other callings.

"I've always been a maker," Whitten told me. "I remember in high school, I was always writing out Bible verses with markers and taping them up to my walls. My walls were covered with Scripture and, of course, the lyrics to my favorite Steven Curtis Chapman and Point of Grace songs."

More than a decade later, with those Bible verse–covered, college-ruled papers collecting dust in the attic of her own household of four, Whitten was inspired to pick "Scripture lettering" back up. "I was looking around my church and the people that I know, and realized that we're just kind of living these humdrum lives. We're not really claiming the effectiveness and the power of Scripture because we simply don't know it. I was reminded of Deuteronomy 6:8–9, where it says, 'You shall bind [these Words] as a sign on your hand, and they shall be as frontlets between your eyes. You shall write them on the doorposts of your house and on your gates' (ESV). That passage brought me back to high school, remembering the Scripture that covered the walls of my bedroom and how visualizing God's Word helped me internalize its truths."

So Whitten set out on a personal experiment to use art to memorize God's Word. "For some reason, Exodus 14:14 came to mind. I spent a lot of time lettering that first verse, so when it was finished, I framed it and hung it in our living room. Every single time I walked into that room, I would see it and repeat the verse back to myself. I quickly realized that the print really helped me memorize and meditate on that verse!"

That's when the Lord gave Whitten a vision for her business to sell hand-lettered Bible verses and teach other women how to produce their own through her Instagram feed (@ KrystalWhitten), workshops, and most recently the *Lettering Prayer Journal*, which Whitten calls "the most important work I've ever done."

Now that she has a rapidly growing business, two children under the age of five, a husband, and responsibilities at church, I asked Whitten the obvious question: "How do you get it all done?"

"I pray that Haven (age three) takes a long nap," she said. "In all seriousness though, it's hard. It's *really* hard. Some days, if she doesn't take her full two-hour nap, I will just let her watch TV so that I can get an hour of work done. I feel really guilty about that. There's a lot of mommy guilt in spending an hour working rather than playing with her."

For Whitten, some of that guilt is self-imposed, but much of it is not. "People from church will ask me to get together for coffee or to get our kids together for a playdate and a lot of times I have to say no. And that's really hard to do, especially when you're a mom running a business from your home. I'll tell these other moms that I have to work and they give me these confused looks as if to say, 'What work?' People really don't understand your work and your decision to follow God's calling on your career in addition to your calling as a mom and wife.

"Just Saturday, my husband and I were sitting outside watching the kids play and I was crying because I felt this weird guilt over feeling like I have a purpose beyond being a wife and mom. I know family comes first always, but where some people want more kids, I want to build a business. I feel like this business is a child and I don't want it to stay in this infant state. I really want it to grow, not for my glory but for the glory of God who has given me this 'child' to care for. I feel like God has given me this talent, he's given me this gift, and for me to just keep it to myself is selfish. I need to share it. I have been called to be a wife. I have been called to be a mom. But I have also been called to create. I feel like this is what I'm supposed to be doing. And if I didn't build this business, I would feel as if I were being a poor steward of the passions, gifts, and opportunities God has given me."

If all callings are equal and all work is inherently good and meaningful because God has ordained it, how are we to discern the specific work God has called us to? Whitten hits the nail on the head: by identifying the passions, giftings, and opportunities God has given us to serve him and others through our work.

3

discerning our calling

Renowned British novelist Dorothy Sayers once said:

> Work is not, primarily, a thing one does to live, but the thing
> one lives to do. It is, or it should be, the full expression of
> the worker's faculties, the thing in which he finds spiritual,
> mental and bodily satisfaction, and the medium in which he
> offers himself to God.[1]

It's hard to take issue with Sayers's assertion that we should
do work that fully expresses our gifts and brings us "spiritual, mental and bodily satisfaction." But to view work as the
means in which we offer ourselves up to God? That sacrificial view of work is almost totally foreign to us today. When
discerning our career paths, almost all of our questions are
aimed at serving ourselves rather than God and others. We
ask, "Which career will earn me the most respect and adoration from others? Which career will help me accumulate the

most wealth in the shortest amount of time? Which career will give me the most freedom and flexibility?"

With questions like these, it's no wonder that a record number of us are choosing the path of entrepreneurship, which holds the promise of coolness, the prospect of riches, and the potential for relative freedom.[2] The fact that all three of these things ultimately come down to our identity is no surprise. For Americans, almost nothing shapes our identity more than our chosen work. It's why "What do you do?" is the first question asked when we meet someone for the first time. Our identities are so wrapped up in our answers to that question that it can feel almost impossible not to choose a career based solely on which job will help us best cultivate the image we want to portray to the world. But as Christians, our identity is already defined. As 1 John 3:1 reminds us, "See what great love the Father has lavished on us, that we should be called children of God! And that is what we are!" We are not what we say we do when introducing ourselves at a party. We are children of God. Because of the gospel, "Our work becomes the expression of our identity and not the source of it."[3]

> Because of the gospel, our work becomes the expression of our identity, not the source of it.

Today, there may be no more glamorous career than that of the entrepreneur. From *Shark Tank* to the rise of rock-star entrepreneurs such as Elon Musk, Jessica Alba, and Mark Cuban, startup fever is everywhere. There's a reason why *The Social Network*,[4] the Academy Award–winning film chronicling the glitzy founding of Facebook, was heralded as the film that "defined a [millennial] generation."[5] It's never been cooler to be an entrepreneur. But cool doesn't equal calling.

Choosing the path of entrepreneurship is obviously not inherently bad. But if our work is going to be more than a job—if it's going to be a true calling on our lives—then we must ask questions not about which career will best boost our self-image but rather how we might best serve the One who has called us to create. The entrepreneurs I interviewed for this book tended to ask three excellent questions when discerning God's calling on their lives:

1. What am I passionate about?
2. What gifts has God given me?
3. Where do I have the greatest opportunity to love others?

What Am I Passionate About?

I first met William Warren in the cafeteria at Chick-fil-A's corporate headquarters in Atlanta, Georgia. As we grabbed our lunch, I couldn't help but think he had a pretty amazing gig (if for no other reason than the fact that he could eat free Chick-fil-A whenever he wanted). Warren was a member of Chick-fil-A's digital marketing team, where he managed the brand's marketing campaigns to millions of email subscribers and social media followers. Like any good Christian raised in the South, he was personally fanatical about Chick-fil-A, which made the job of talking about the company and its products a lot of fun. From an outsider's point of view, William Warren had a dream job.

That's why I was so surprised when he called me a few months later to tell me that he was leaving Chick-fil-A. The fact that Chick-fil-A's corporate turnover rate is so low (about 5 percent) made me even more intrigued to hear why he had decided to make the leap.[6] He explained that he loved working at Chick-fil-A, the people he worked with, and the generous compensation of the job. "But did you know I am a trained cartoonist?" he asked.

The question caught me off-guard. He explained that ever since he could hold a pencil, he had been drawing comic strips and editorial cartoons. "When I was in high school, I would sit in class and draw in the margins of my textbooks, creating my own animated flip-books." Years later, he showed me one of these textbooks, flipping through the pages to reveal a scene of an army tank invading a town. Illustration had clearly been a passion for Warren throughout his life.

"While I loved my work at Chick-fil-A," he continued, "I have always wanted to start a business where I could combine my passions for illustration and communicating big ideas." In the words of Sayers, Warren wasn't finding total "spiritual, mental and bodily satisfaction" in his work at Chick-fil-A. Months before our conversation, he had discovered the growing practice of "graphic recording," where an illustrator listens to a speaker at an event and, in real time, sketches images and text that summarize the speaker's message, creating a visual artifact of the talk. Warren quickly taught himself these skills and began using them to record internal meetings at Chick-fil-A and sermons for his pastor, Andy Stanley. From there, business requests started pouring in, allowing him to leave Chick-fil-A to launch The Sketch Effect, an Atlanta-based visual communications agency that has now done work for other top-tier brands such as Google, Nike, the NBA, Delta, Ernst & Young, and Mattress Firm.[7] The business is growing like a weed, and Warren has never been happier.

As we have already explored, God appears to have created for the pure joy of creating. He created because he wanted to, not because he needed to. Isaiah 64:8 reminds us that "We are the clay, and [God] our potter" (ESV). One of the ways God molds us and helps us discern our calling is by giving us our passions, the things that bring us pure joy. The fact that you are reading this book suggests you are passionate about entrepreneurship and creativity. Identifying passions like these is key to discerning our calling, but passion without competence is worthless.

What Gifts Has God Given Me?

Writing to the early church in Rome, the apostle Paul said, "Since we have gifts that differ according to the grace given to us, each of us is to exercise them accordingly" (Rom. 12:6 NASB). We have largely ignored this verse in the church today, choosing to define calling as simply what we are really passionate about, rather than the intersection of our passions and giftings. We see this in the church all the time. A woman "feels called" to sing on the praise team, and the worship leader lets her, even though he knows she can't carry a tune. So she hops up on stage and the worship leader turns her microphone off so nobody can hear her. Rather than lovingly being redirected to an activity in the church where she can actually be of service to others, the woman spends years singing her heart out, serving only herself and her "passion."

> In order to best glorify our Creator and love others, Christians should do the work God has equipped us to do exceptionally well.

In order to best glorify our Creator and love others, Christians should do the work we are best at, work that God has equipped us to do exceptionally well. As Sayers points out in her classic essay, "Why Work?":

> The Church's approach to an intelligent carpenter is usually confined to exhorting him not to be drunk and disorderly in his leisure hours, and to come to church on Sundays. What the Church should be telling him is this: that the very first demand that his religion makes upon him is that he should make good tables.[8]

Sayers is calling Christians to exercise what pastor Timothy Keller calls the "ministry of competence."[9] If we choose work we can't do well, that's a poor reflection on God, whose character we are called to image to the world. Likewise, in order to love our neighbor through our work, we must be competent in our chosen field.

"The maid who sweeps her kitchen is doing the will of God just as much as the monk who prays—not because she may sing a Christian hymn as she sweeps but because God loves clean floors. The Christian shoemaker does his duty not by putting little crosses on the shoes, but by making good shoes, because God is interested in good craftsmanship." This quote, often attributed to Martin Luther, illustrates the ministry of competence well, especially when read in line with the fact that "Luther's doctrine of vocation is the insistence that work is done in service of the neighbor and of the world. God likes shoes (and good ones!) not for their own sake, but because the neighbor needs shoes."[10] One of the primary ways we love our neighbor is by doing work we are gifted at. In *Culture Making*, Andy Crouch argues that, when discerning our calling:

> The right question is whether, when we undertake the work we believe to be our vocation, we experience the joy and humility that come only when God multiplies our work so that it bears thirty, sixty and a hundredfold beyond what we could expect from our feeble inputs. Vocation—calling—becomes another word for a continual process of discernment, examining the fruits of our work to see whether they are producing that kind of fruit, and doing all we can to scatter the next round of seed in the most fruitful places.[11]

We don't enter our careers knowing what we will be exceptionally good at. It takes trial and error to discover the gifts God has given us. And individual failures don't necessarily mean we aren't gifted in a particular field. Tom Brady, quarterback for the New England Patriots and three-time Super Bowl MVP, only completes 63.5 percent of his passes. That means that one of the greatest NFL quarterbacks of all time fails 36.5 percent of the time. Yet Brady is anything but a failure. Failure is relative to the field you are in. In entrepreneurship, failure is more common than success. A single failure doesn't necessarily mean that you haven't been called to create, but you should be in a "continual process of discernment," on the lookout for patterns and listening to the counsel of others to identify the gifts God has given you.

In 2014, I began making plans to transition out of the day-to-day operations of Citizinvestor, the company I cofounded in 2012. Around this time, my church hosted a guest speaker who spoke about the need to plant churches in major cities across the United States. As I sat listening to the presentation, I began to sense that God might be calling me and my family to plant a church in Washington, DC. My wife and I are passionate about the gospel, cities, and Washington specifically, so we could quickly check off the "passion" box in discerning God's calling. But we weren't sure we would be any good at planting a church. I reasoned to myself, thinking *I'm gifted in launching and growing businesses, so maybe I should be applying those skills to planting a church.*

As I talked through this idea with friends and mentors, however, many of them said something to this effect: "If you know you are a gifted entrepreneur, why in the world would you not continue applying those skills to, you know, the world of entrepreneurship and business?" In retrospect, my friends' advice seems so obvious. But it wasn't at the time. At that point in my career, God had given me clear validation that he had equipped me with the gifts needed to be a competent entrepreneur, gifts he had used to allow me to love and serve others. While those gifts would have certainly applied to the process of planting a church, I knew they were applicable in the arena in which God had already placed me. So instead of starting a church, I felt God calling me to start another business (Vocreo) where I could share my God-given gifts with other entrepreneurs, helping them fulfill their call to create.

Discerning the gifts God has given us takes some experimentation and failure, especially if you are exploring the path of entrepreneurship. But while all work will deal its share of frustrations and failures, it is up to each of us to honestly ask if the work we are doing is the work God has equipped us to do well, to best glorify him and love others.

Where Do I Have the Greatest Opportunity to Love Others?

While some of us may have the passion and aptitude for entrepreneurship, not everyone has been given clear opportunities to use those gifts to love and serve others. Maybe you simply haven't had an idea for a product or service that you think will genuinely serve others. Or maybe it's something more difficult to change: finances, family obligations, your health, or the health of a loved one.

The first time I met Chris Johnson, he had just quit a good job to start his first business. I was excited for him! He clearly had a passion for entrepreneurship, proven skills that would be useful for a first-time founder, and an idea for a product that would serve others well. Shortly after the launch of the business, his wife, Jamie, gave birth to their first child. In the midst of their joy, their doctors delivered some unsettling news: their daughter was born with a hole in her heart and would need open-heart surgery. Starting a business and having a baby at the same time is borderline crazy, as I can personally attest.[12] Add to that the stress of your first child being born with a serious medical condition, and most people would find the stress overwhelming.

"It was really hard to focus on anything else during that time," Johnson shared with me in retrospect. "Of course, I needed to keep working, but I knew I couldn't devote the focus necessary to make our startup work while also fulfilling my responsibilities as a husband and father."

At the onset of his entrepreneurial endeavor, Johnson saw a clear opportunity to launch a new business. But with the convergence of these life events, Johnson no longer felt that his family could afford the financial risk of him starting a new, capitally intensive venture. For the moment, Johnson's window of opportunity was closing, so he and his partner made the decision to put their startup on hold. The world might call Johnson foolish, tell him to hustle harder, take out a second mortgage, or simply suck it up. But I think he was incredibly brave because he was humble enough to put aside his pride and ambitions to see where God was moving in his life. At that moment in Johnson's life, for reasons he didn't understand, he was not called to create in the way he had originally intended.

Blake Mycoskie's story is entirely different. Before becoming the founder and "Chief Shoe Giver" of TOMS, Mycoskie had already proven his passion and aptitude for entrepreneurship. He started his first company, a laundry delivery service for college students called EZ Laundry, while he was a sophomore at Southern Methodist University. Within one year, the business had grown to more than $1,000,000 in sales with more than forty employees. That's when Mycoskie realized he was wired to be an entrepreneur and dropped out of school. He recounts, "I realized I loved doing this. I realized I loved the idea of creating something out of scratch and seeing it work."[13] After selling EZ Laundry to a partner, Mycoskie continued putting his entrepreneurial skills to work, launching businesses as diverse as an outdoor billboard company that marketed country music (acquired by Clear Channel), to an all-reality cable TV channel, to an online service that taught teenagers driver's education.[14]

But all of these ventures pale in comparison to TOMS Shoes, the company responsible for turning Mycoskie into the poster child for social entrepreneurship. While a contestant on season two of the hit CBS reality TV show *The Amazing*

Race, Mycoskie and his sister Paige sprinted across the globe. On their journey, they quickly passed through Argentina, where Mycoskie got a taste of the country and vowed to return. In 2006, he made good on that promise, taking a much-needed vacation to Argentina and immersing himself in the culture. As he explains, part of this cultural immersion included "wearing the national shoe: the alpargata, a soft, casual canvas shoe worn by almost everyone in the country, from polo players to farmers to students. An idea began to form in the back of my mind: Maybe the alpargata would have some market appeal in the United States."[15] Toward the end of his trip, Mycoskie met a team of Americans who had collected donated shoes in the United States for shoeless children in Argentina. He was intrigued and followed the team around to learn more about the problem of shoelessness. "It was heartbreaking," Mycoskie says. "I spent a few days traveling from village to village, and a few more traveling on my own, witnessing the intense pockets of poverty just outside the bustling capital. It dramatically heightened my awareness. Yes, I knew somewhere in the back of my mind that poor children around the world often went barefoot, but now, for the first time, I saw the real effects of being shoeless: the blisters, the sores, the infections—all the result of the children not being able to protect their young feet from the ground."[16]

Mycoskie saw a problem he wanted to solve. But how? "My parents always engaged us in community service through our church," he recalls, but he knew the nonprofit model of conducting shoe drives was unsustainable.[17] Through his experience as a successful entrepreneur, Mycoskie knew that he had "been given entrepreneurial gifts."[18] With this in mind, he says, "I began to look for solutions in the world I already knew: business and entrepreneurship."[19] The solution was TOMS Shoes, a for-profit company that promised to match every pair of shoes purchased with a new pair of shoes given to a child in need. Since the founding of TOMS in 2006, the company has given away more than sixty million pairs of shoes to children in need[20] all around the world and built a business worth $625 million.[21]

For Mycoskie, "building [TOMS] is a theological mandate. He frames his Christian faith as a component of his personal relationship to the company."[22] At a conference hosted by Willow Creek Church,[23] Mycoskie said, "I remember sitting in church my freshman year in college thinking that I would work really hard to be a very successful entrepreneur and make a ton of money so that later in my life, in my sixties or seventies, I could spend my time giving it away. And I knew that I would be really blessed by that."[24] But then he realized that entrepreneurship itself could be used to serve God, not just by donating profits to charity. In a book titled *Work as Worship*, Mycoskie shared, "In a sense, [TOMS has] allowed me to go into ministry without having to leave my passion for entrepreneurialism."[25]

It's clear in retrospect that God used Mycoskie's vacation in Argentina to present a great opportunity for him to love and serve his neighbors all around the globe. He clearly had a passion for entrepreneurship, a giftedness for the craft, and a golden opportunity to love and serve millions of people. Like William Warren and myself, Mycoskie was clearly called to create.

But what would have happened had any of these entrepreneurs not answered God's call? In Matthew 25, Jesus seems to suggest that any such non-response would constitute poor stewardship:

> Again, it will be like a man going on a journey, who called his servants and entrusted his wealth to them. To one he gave five bags of gold, to another two bags, and to another one bag, each according to his ability. Then he went on his journey. The man who had received five bags of gold went at once and put his money to work and gained five bags more. So also, the one with two bags of gold gained two more. But the man who had received one bag went off, dug a hole in the ground and hid his master's money.
>
> After a long time the master of those servants returned and settled accounts with them. The man who had received five bags of gold brought the other five. "Master," he said, "you entrusted me with five bags of gold. See, I have gained five more."
>
> His master replied, "Well done, good and faithful servant! You have been faithful with a few things; I will put you in charge of many things. Come and share your master's happiness!"
>
> The man with two bags of gold also came. "Master," he said, "you entrusted me with two bags of gold; see, I have gained two more."
>
> His master replied, "Well done, good and faithful servant! You have been faithful with a few things; I will put you in charge of many things. Come and share your master's happiness!"
>
> Then the man who had received one bag of gold came. "Master," he said, "I knew that you are a hard man, harvesting where you have not sown and gathering where you have not scattered seed. So I was afraid and went out and hid your gold in the ground. See, here is what belongs to you."

His master replied, "You wicked, lazy servant! So you knew that I harvest where I have not sown and gather where I have not scattered seed? Well then, you should have put my money on deposit with the bankers, so that when I returned I would have received it back with interest. So take the bag of gold from him and give it to the one who has ten bags. For whoever has will be given more, and they will have an abundance. Whoever does not have, even what they have will be taken from them. And throw that worthless servant outside, into the darkness, where there will be weeping and gnashing of teeth." (Matt. 25:14–30)

As Reverend Robert Sirico points out, "There seems to be a natural connection between the discovery of entrepreneurial opportunities and the master's admonition in Matthew 25 to be watchful of his return and to be caretakers of his property."[26] If you are passionate about entrepreneurship, gifted at the craft, and have been given opportunities to use those passions and gifts to love and serve others, you are called to create. Now it's up to you to steward those God-given gifts well, so that one day the Master might also say to you, "Well done, good and faithful servant."

> Our work can only be a calling if God calls us to it and we work for his sake and not our own.

If you are still reading this book, it is likely that God has indeed called you to create. But unless you reimagine your work not as a means of glorifying yourself but as service to the One who has called you, your work will never feel like more than a job. It will never feel like a true calling on your life. Our work can only be a calling if God calls us to it and we work for his sake and not our

64

own. How does reimagining our work as service to God and others shape our motivations for creating, the products we choose to create, and how we build our organizations? Those are the questions we turn to in part 2 of this book.

PART 2

creating

4

why we create

As you approach the gates to Disney's Magic Kingdom, you begin to sense that you are entering an idyllic world. The sidewalks are spotless. There's no trash in sight. Every flower is in full bloom. The uniform of every "cast member" is perfectly pressed. Just thirty minutes ago, you were driving past dilapidated billboards and cheap motels along central Florida's Interstate 4. But here at Disney, it feels as if you are stepping into an entirely different and more perfect world. If it wasn't for the child throwing a temper tantrum because his mom didn't buy him a Mickey Mouse ice cream bar, you might mistake this for paradise.

Disney's Magic Kingdom is a good thing. It is also a tremendous success. In recent years, the Magic Kingdom (just one of twelve Disney theme parks) has welcomed almost twenty million people per year from all around the world.[1] It is no wonder that Walt Disney is one of the most respected entrepreneurs of our time. From humble beginnings in the

American Midwest, Disney worked tirelessly to bring his visions to life, first with an animation studio and then with the theme parks that continue to bear his name more than fifty years after his death.

If Disney created something new for the good of others, did his motivations for doing so matter? The Bible tells us in Proverbs 16:2 that "All a person's ways seem pure to them, but motives are weighed by the LORD." To God, motives matter a great deal. So why did Disney create? What motivated him to build his entertainment empire? As with any human being, the evidence suggests that his motives were mixed. When his daughters Diane and Sharon were young, he would spend hours watching them circle on the merry-go-round at Griffith Park in Los Angeles. Disney thought the park was filthy, and once commented to a friend, "One of these days I'm going to build an amusement park—and it's going to be clean!" Reminiscing about her father, Diane Disney noted another of her father's motivations to build theme parks: "He'd see families in the park and say, 'There's nothing for the parents to do. . . . You've got to have a place where the whole family can have fun.'"[2]

> To God, motives matter a great deal.

Disney's motivations to create a clean, safe place where families could come to have fun together were good. But when one looks at the entirety of Disney's life and career, it's clear that these weren't his primary motivations for creating. Disney's life, like that of most entrepreneurs today, appears to have been lived to make a name for himself. In 1966, Walt's brother Roy was planning on retiring from the company he and his brother had built. But after Walt's death, Roy had a change of heart:

Roy realized there was one last way he could look out for his brother, by protecting the thing that Walt cared more about than his health or his finances—his name. He called off retirement. Roy would stick around until the first phase of Walt's final dream was completed, with the new name of *Walt* Disney World, so people would always remember whose world this was.[3]

To this day, everything in the Disney empire points back to the company's creator. Every product bears his name and signature. Even Disneyland and its sister theme park the Magic Kingdom—the crowning achievements of Disney's career—were designed by Disney to serve as a monument to his life and legacy. As Neal Gabler explains in his biography of Disney:

[Disneyland] was a reflection of its creator and his own over-weening sense of wish fulfillment. But it reflected him in a much more personal way as well. By formulating the park with a walk down Main Street at the park's entrance, which led to Sleeping Beauty Castle at the street's end and then to the various lands that radiated from the castle (Fantasyland, Adventureland, Frontierland, and Tomorrowland), Walt Disney recreated his own life's journey: "the road map of Walt Disney's life," as [Disney] veteran Marty Sklar would describe it. One entered the gates of the park into what was essentially the Main Street of Walt's boyhood Marceline [Kansas]. (At "story sessions" for Disneyland he would reminisce about Marceline by the hour.) At the end of the street one was offered a variety of options—fantasy, adventure, the frontier, the future—so that a trip through the park became a metaphor for possibility. Like young Walt, visitors to the castle seemed to stand at the portal to their dreams with a

71

child's sense of omnipotence. "The symbolism," Richard Schickel would write, "is almost too perfect—the strangers forced to recapitulate Disney's formative experiences before being allowed to visit his fancies and fantasies in other areas of the Magic Kingdom."[4]

Walt Disney designed a world that would reflect him. If the symbolic design of the park doesn't make this clear enough, the next time you visit the Magic Kingdom, walk down any path until you reach the center of the park. There, at the center of the world he created, you will find a statue of Walt Disney, a not-so-subtle reminder that this world was designed by him and for his glory. Walt Disney, more than maybe any entrepreneur in the last century, succeeded in fulfilling the often unspoken dream of most of us today: to make a name for ourselves. But the Bible shows us that this dream is nothing new. In fact, it is something those who are called to create have been wrestling with since the near beginning of time.

Making a Name for Ourselves

In Genesis 11, we are introduced to the people of Babel, who had discovered a major technical innovation: brick making. With the invention of the brick-making process, the entrepreneurial Babylonians could now build better homes, roads, and cities—all wonderful things; but motivated by pride, the Babylonians also saw an opportunity to use this technology to make a name for themselves:

> Now the whole world had one language and a common speech. As people moved eastward, they found a plain in Shinar and settled there. They said to each other, "Come,

let's make bricks and bake them thoroughly." They used brick instead of stone, and tar for mortar. Then they said, "Come, let us build ourselves a city, with a tower that reaches to the heavens, so that we may make a name for ourselves; otherwise we will be scattered over the face of the whole earth." But the LORD came down to see the city and the tower the people were building. The LORD said, "If as one people speaking the same language they have begun to do this, then nothing they plan to do will be impossible for them. Come, let us go down and confuse their language so they will not understand each other." So the LORD scattered them from there over all the earth, and they stopped building the city. That is why it was called Babel—because there the LORD confused the language of the whole world. From there the LORD scattered them over the face of the whole earth. (Gen. 11:1–9)

Creating a tower or a theme park is not an inherently bad thing. Towers and theme parks can and do reveal God's character and love for others. But when we create something out of a motivation to make a name for ourselves or to "make our mark" on the world, we, like Walt Disney and the Babylonians, are attempting to rob God of the glory that is rightfully his. As pastor John Piper says, commenting on this passage in Genesis 11, "God's will for human beings is not that we find our joy in being praised, but that we find our joy in knowing and praising him."[5]

> When we create to make a name for ourselves, we are attempting to rob God of the glory that is rightfully his.

The world offers many motivations for entrepreneurs: money, power, status, and influence are just a few. But all of these motivations can be summed up in this deep-seated desire to make a name for ourselves. At our core, we know there is something deeply wrong with us and we work insanely hard to prove to the world that we are not a chump. To prove that we are valuable. To prove that our life is meaningful. The beautiful truth of the gospel is that Jesus Christ has done all of that work for us! As a Christian who believes that God came to earth as a human to die for you, you can rest knowing that you are somebody, because you have been adopted as a child of God. You can rest knowing that you are valuable, because God gave up his only Son to ransom you. You can rest knowing that your life has meaning, because God has made you a new creation and has called you to use your passions, gifts, and opportunities to reveal his character and love others. Following the call to create means that we no longer work to make a name for ourselves; we work for the glory of the One who has called us. In the words of the apostle Paul, "Whatever you do, do it all for the glory of God" (1 Cor. 10:31).

> Following the call to create means that we no longer work to make a name for ourselves; we work for the glory of the One who has called us.

Hannah Brencher had to learn these lessons the hard way. At first glance, Brencher's story appears to be the stuff movies are made of. After graduating from college, Brencher moved to New York City, where she struggled to adjust to life in the big city. Instead of sulking in self-pity, Brencher turned her pain into motivation for loving complete strangers. "I found myself ripping encouraging letters out of my notebook and leaving them all over New York City for people to find," Brencher shared. "I left them everywhere: coffee shops, libraries, coat pockets in department stores. I liked to imagine who might find those letters. Somehow that idea took on a life of its own after I blogged about it. My inbox was filled with the most heartbreaking stories I've ever encountered after I published a simple question on my blog: 'Do you need someone to write you a love letter today? Just ask.' That one question changed my life forever as I spent the next year writing hundreds of love letters to strangers in all parts of the world."

Following Brencher's social experiment, she founded More Love Letters, what she described as "A global organization using the power behind social media to handwrite and mail letters to individuals in need around the world." As her organization grew, so did Brencher's star power. At the age of twenty-four, she took the stage at TED, one of the world's most elite conferences, and the video of her talk quickly surpassed one million views. Brencher rapidly racked up speaking requests, email subscribers, and Twitter followers and even secured a book deal to write her memoir. By the world's standards, Brencher had made it.

But if you saw Brencher walking down the crowded streets of New York City on March 9, 2015, you would never have guessed this was her story. On the eve of her book's release, Brencher was walking aimlessly around Manhattan with tears in her eyes. As Brencher said, "This was supposed to be the most meaningful, awesome, inspirational time of my life, but I just remember walking around New York City bawling my eyes out saying, 'God, this is not what I thought this was going to look like.'" Brencher was entering the deepest depression of her life. Over the next few weeks, Brencher had to fight to get out of bed, lost ten pounds, and was even admitted to the hospital.

Looking back, Brencher can see the source of her depression: she had placed her identity in the name she was making for herself, not in the One who had called her to create. As she recalled, "When the book was done, I didn't know where to put my worth, I didn't know where to put my identity, I didn't know where to put my sixteen-hour days that I had been giving to this thing for the last seven months. I lost my life to my book. Timothy Keller says, 'If you love anything in this world more than God, you will crush that object under the weight of your expectations.' Whether it's a book, or a company, or a mission, or whatever it is, it couldn't be truer than that. I had to learn through my depression that the book wasn't going to give me worth; More Love Letters didn't give me worth. I had to get to the point where I could say, 'God, you are enough.'"

In retrospect, Brencher is grateful for this dark time in her life and sees how God has used it for his glory and her good. "It's hard in the world we live in not to want to make a name for yourself," Brencher shared. "Everyone is telling you that you need to have a Twitter account, that you need to have a personal brand, that you need to have a blog. God can use those things to allow us to be a vessel for him, but we can get so swept up in the name game that we forget why we should be creating: to make much of him. We need to be willing to assume the role God has called us to, no matter if the role is ever seen, or ever announced on Twitter, or ever included in the *Wall Street Journal*. The end goal is not getting credit from people, it's getting to be a part of what the Creator has ordained."

As Brencher experienced, the gospel replaces worldly motivations with motivations to serve God and others. While

I certainly do not presume to know why all-powerful God created the world and humankind, as we saw in the first chapter of this book the creation account in Genesis provides us with some clues. God appears to have created the world and humankind for two primary reasons: to reveal his character and to love others. As we look to displace the world's motivations for creating, looking to the motives of the One who has called us to create seems like the most logical place to start. As we adopt the First Entrepreneur's motivations as our own, our work takes on an entirely different and richer meaning, bringing deep satisfaction as we create to reveal our Creator's character and love others.

Soli Deo Gloria

Johann Sebastian Bach sensed God calling him to create at an early age. Bach grew up in a town not far from where Martin Luther birthed the Protestant Reformation, a place where "Luther was a great deal more compelling than gravity."[6] His family surrounded him with love, Lutheranism, and music—the sounds of violins, organs, and choruses constantly filled his life. It didn't take long for the family to recognize young Bach's exceptional musical talents. His father, uncle, and other family members encouraged and developed these giftings by giving Bach his first music lessons. Tragically, Bach's parents would never see the full fruits of their investment in Bach on this side of eternity. Before Bach's tenth birthday, he was an orphan. After his mother and father died, Bach moved in with a family member and continued honing his musical skills and Lutheran theology.

As Bach entered the workforce, he knew precisely what he felt God was calling him to do: to marry his love of music and theology to achieve his "goal of a well-regulated church music"—defined by Bach as a series of cantatas (fifteen- to thirty-minute narrative pieces of music) for all Sundays and Feast Days of the church year. With his appointment as cantor (eighteenth-century speak for "worship leader") of Leipzig, Bach was given an opportunity to pursue his life's work. And "he pursued it with unimaginable energy," composing nearly 120 cantatas in his first two years on the job.[7] He accomplished this incredible feat while also fulfilling his duties as a music teacher and performer at his church. Even with Bach's extraordinary work ethic, he managed to lead a growing family of twenty children and maintain two consecutive happy marriages (his first wife passed away just before Bach's move to Leipzig).

What motivated Bach to work with such "unimaginable energy"? Bach had reimagined his creating not as a means of making a name for himself; instead, Bach believed that "The aim and final end of all music should be none other than the glory of God and the refreshment of the soul." In a well-researched profile on Bach in *Christian History* magazine, the author points out that:

> A well-regulated church music was not the whole of Bach's vocation. His larger calling was writing music to the glory of God and the edification of his neighbor. This, as the historian Jaroslav Pelikan wrote, "bespeaks the conviction of Luther and the Reformers that the performance of any God-pleasing vocation was the service of God."[8]

While today we recognize Bach as one of the greatest composers who ever lived, his work wasn't celebrated until long after his death. But the lack of recognition didn't appear to faze him. At the end of his compositions, Bach inscribed the Latin phrase *Soli Deo Gloria*, meaning "Glory to God alone"—a reminder to Bach and history of why he created and whose recognition he sought.

In the middle of writing this chapter, I underwent a routine surgical operation. As the nurse was rolling up my sleeve to take my blood pressure before surgery, I caught myself thinking about the words to a song that had been stuck in my head for days. No, it wasn't a Bach cantata I was singing; it was a song about another eighteenth-century orphan made famous by his exceptional writings: Alexander Hamilton. The song was from the hit musical *Hamilton*, which, since making its debut in 2015, has blown critics and fans away (myself included).[9] What in the world does a hip-hop musical about Alexander Hamilton and the founding of the United States have to do with our motivations for creating? Stick with me for one more minute.

What makes the musical so compelling (besides the joy of watching George Washington, Thomas Jefferson, and others rap their way through the American Revolution) is the lesser-known but fascinating story of Hamilton, "the ten-dollar founding father" and America's first secretary of the treasury. Hamilton grew up fatherless and poor in the Caribbean. At the age of twelve, his mother died in his arms, leaving him, like Bach, orphaned at an early age. Following his mother's death, Hamilton moved in with a cousin, who soon after committed suicide. As if this orphan's story wasn't tragic enough, in 1772 a hurricane devastated Hamilton's hometown. A self-educated teenager, Hamilton wrote a detailed account of the storm that was published in the local paper. Upon reading his story, Hamilton's neighbors were amazed at his talents as a writer. They raised enough money to book him a ticket out of the Caribbean on a ship bound for New York City, promising the young revolutionary that "The world's going to know your name!" When Hamilton walks onto the staged streets of New York City for the first time, he publicly vows an ascent to greatness that will ensure the history books remember him. This is Hamilton's declaration of significance.

Unlike Bach, who created for the glory of God alone, Hamilton was driven by a desire to glorify himself. This motivation to make a name for himself is a major theme of his life and the musical. His idolatry of his work leads him to neglect his family, cheat on his wife, and publicize details of his extramarital affair in a misguided attempt to protect his legacy as a politician. In a song titled "Non-Stop,"[10] which highlights Hamilton's unrivaled work ethic, the chorus asks him most poignantly: "Why do you write like you're running out of time?"

> If we see our creating as a means of revealing God's character and loving others, then we have proper ambition to create like we are running out of time, because, in fact, we are!

This was the lyric that caught my attention as I sat with the blood pressure sleeve choking the life out of my arm. *Why did Hamilton write like he was running out of time?* I wondered. Like most of us, he was doing it to make a name for himself, to glorify himself, to leave a legacy. Hamilton's work ethic was not the problem, though. Colossians 3:23 says "Whatever you do, work at it with all your heart." Both Bach and Hamilton clearly worked with all of their hearts.

The difference in their stories is *why* they worked like they were running out of time. The difference is one of motivation. The second half of Colossians 3:23 says "[Work] for the Lord, not for human masters." And therein lies the key. If we create to make a name for ourselves, we will never be satisfied. We will never feel as if our work is more than a job, a true calling on our lives. And, inevitably, we will devastate our lives and those of our loved ones. But if we, like Bach, see our creating as a means of revealing God's character and loving others, then we have proper ambition to write, work, and create like we are running out of time—because, in fact, we are!

Everyone knows the cliché that nobody lies on their death-bed wishing they had spent more time at the office. While imminent death certainly clarifies what is and what is not important in life, this cliché is based on the myth we have already debunked that work is inherently bad and meaning-less. By adopting God's motivations for creating as your own, can you envision yourself on your deathbed wishing you *had* spent more time using your entrepreneurial skills and creativity to reveal God's character and love others?

As I was lying in my hospital bed, waiting to be wheeled into surgery, I asked myself, *Why am I not writing like I'm running out of time?* We are *all* running out of time. Sure, on that day I was just having a routine operation, but one day I will likely be lying in a hospital bed knowing that the end of my life is near. And because I know I have been called to create, I *will* write, work, and create like I am running out of time today, so that I don't look back with regret wishing I had spent more time working to reveal God's character and love others.

5

what we create

As we saw in the previous chapter, following God's call to create replaces our motivation to make a name for ourselves with motivation to create in order to reveal God's character and love others. Like oxygen to the body, motivations impact every aspect of an entrepreneurial endeavor, but they manifest themselves perhaps most poignantly in the products we choose to create.

Dave Blanchard is the founder and CEO of Praxis, an accelerator for Christian-led startups. Standing on a stage in front of dozens of Christian entrepreneurs and investors in Silicon Valley, Blanchard eloquently called for "an alternative imagination" for those who are called to create.[1] As Blanchard argued, entrepreneurs are trained to evaluate ideas almost solely based on their viability. "If somebody says, 'That's a good idea,' they are saying, 'That would work.' If it's a business, that would make a lot of money. If it's a nonprofit, you could raise money for that," he said.[2] Blanchard argued that the entrepreneurial ecosystem has taught us to think exclusively in terms of product market fit, where the only question is whether or not there's a market willing to buy a particular product. "Generally speaking, entrepreneurs attempt to figure out where the world is going, and leverage those trends to considerable financial gain," Blanchard said. "Could our aim [as Christian entrepreneurs] be for more? Disrupting negative cultural trends and encouraging positive emerging trends with innovative, transformative, gospel-minded ventures?"[3]

What Blanchard is calling for is a focus on what he calls "impact market fit," which leads us to begin our search for products to create with questions not about viability but about what is on God's heart. As Abraham Kuyper famously said, that list is practically infinite: "There is not a square inch in the whole domain of our human existence over which Christ, who is Sovereign over all, does not cry, Mine!"[4]

How should we, as Christian entrepreneurs, think differently about what we create? As we have already explored, our work is only a calling if we do it for the sake of the One who has called us. Thus, we should begin the process of discerning what to create with questions about our Caller. In the words of Andy Crouch:

> For Christians, calling does not fundamentally begin with questions about ourselves but about God. Like the Pevensie children in C. S. Lewis' Narnia chronicles, we will very likely find ourselves suddenly snatched from a known and comfortable world to another one, where extraordinary things are expected of us that seem far beyond our own talents and capabilities. But as the Pevensies learn, what matters at those times is not so much what they bring to Narnia's moment of cultural crisis as that "Aslan is on the move."[5]

God is always moving around us. Through prayer, study of his Word, and fellowship with other believers, he often reveals to us where he is moving and how we might join him in his work, creating products that will reveal his character and love others.

Create Products That Reveal God's Character

At first glance, authors might not look like entrepreneurs, but they actually fit quite nicely within our definition of "anyone who takes a risk to create something new for the good of others." Take C. S. Lewis, for example. Time and time again, Lewis took reputational and financial risk to share his writings with the world, and he certainly created something new for the good of others. He created entire worlds with his words, which have captured the imagination of millions of fans.

> For Christians, calling does not fundamentally begin with questions about ourselves but about God.

Until age thirty-three, Lewis was an atheist already on his way to a successful career as an academic and author. In 1925, he was elected a fellow of Magdalen College in Oxford, where he taught English language and literature. Six years later, Lewis became a Christian. But Lewis's newfound faith didn't change the trajectory of his career; it didn't inspire him to leave Magdalen College, where he continued to teach for another twenty-three years. It did, however, heavily influence what he created.

Today, Lewis is remembered as one of the twentieth century's most influential Christian theologians, bringing great logic and depth of understanding to the faith of millions of

Christ-followers. But this is only because, after his conversion to Christianity, Lewis used his gifts to create products that revealed the character of God. Through works such as *Mere Christianity*, *The Screwtape Letters*, and *The Four Loves*, Lewis used words to paint pictures of who God is and who he is not. The best example of this is found in Lewis's most popular work, The Chronicles of Narnia, a children's fiction series that tells the stories of four children and their epic adventures through a magical land called Narnia. Since its release in 1950, the series of seven books has sold more than one hundred million copies in forty-seven languages.[6] Few fictional series in the past century have been more beloved, especially by Christians who appreciate both the subtle and not-so-subtle revelations of God's character through the stories, especially in the character of Aslan, the Christ-like lion who creates Narnia and redeems it through his sacrificial death.

Perhaps contrary to popular belief, Lewis, like most entrepreneurs, did not lock himself in a room until he came up with an idea for a product that would reveal God's character. As he explained:

> Some people seem to think that I began by asking myself how I could say something about Christianity to children; then fixed on the fairy tale as an instrument, then collected information about child psychology and decided what age group I'd write for; then drew up a list of basic Christian truths and hammered out "allegories" to embody them. This is all pure moonshine. I couldn't write in that way.
>
> All my seven Narnian books began with seeing pictures in my head. At first they were not a story, just pictures. [*The Lion, the Witch and the Wardrobe*] began with a picture of a Faun carrying an umbrella and parcels in a snowy wood. This

picture had been in my mind since I was about sixteen. Then one day, when I was about forty, I said to myself: "Let's try to make a story about it." At first I had very little idea how the story would go. But then suddenly Aslan came bounding into it . . . once he was there he pulled the whole story together.[7]

I would submit that "Aslan came bounding into" the story because Lewis had let the "true Aslan," Jesus Christ, come bounding into his life. Lewis's faith was genuine. He studied Scripture, regularly attended St. Mary Magdalen's Church in Oxford, gave generously to the poor, and surrounded himself in regular fellowship with other believers like J. R. R. Tolkien and other members of "the Inklings" (whom you'll learn more about in chapter 9).

Narnia, and Lewis's other works, may have started with pictures in his head. But it's clear that, as the stories developed, Lewis shaped the books to become a vehicle for revealing God's character. Like Jesus, Lewis saw parables as a powerful means of revealing spiritual truths. In a letter to a fan in 1961, Lewis wrote:

The whole Narnian story is about Christ. That is to say, I asked myself "Supposing that there really was a world like Narnia and supposing it had (like our world) gone wrong and supposing Christ wanted to go into that world and save it (as he did ours), what might have happened?" The stories are my answers. Since Narnia is a world of Talking Beasts, I thought he would become a Talking Beast there, as he became a man here. I pictured Him becoming a lion there because (a) the lion is supposed to be the king of beasts; (b) Christ is called "The Lion of Judah" in the Bible; (c) I'd been having strange dreams about lions when I began writing the work. The whole series works out like this.

The Magician's Nephew tells the Creation and how evil entered Narnia.

The Lion, the Witch and the Wardrobe, the Crucifixion and Resurrection.

Prince Caspian, restoration of the true religion after corruption.

The Horse and His Boy, the calling and conversion of a heathen.

The Voyage of the Dawn Treader, the spiritual life (especially in Reepicheep).

The Silver Chair, the continuing war with the powers of darkness.

The Last Battle, the coming of the Antichrist (the Ape), the end of the world, and the Last Judgment.[8]

Like Lewis, our product ideas will likely not come from brainstorming sessions where we focus intensely on how we can create a product that reveals God's character. But as we begin to create and "let the Word of Christ dwell in [us] richly" (Col. 3:16 ESV), we will undoubtedly see how we can use our creations to reveal the character of the One we adore. Lewis's salvation didn't change his work; it changed his relation *to* his work. His faith provided new motivations for creating and focused the products he wrote on what would reveal the character of the One who called him to create.

But creating to reveal God's character doesn't mean we must create products that are overtly evangelical. Take Citizinvestor, for example. When my cofounders and I launched our crowdfunding platform for government projects in 2012, we didn't have an explicitly evangelical product or mission. Our mission was to empower citizens to invest in their communities by donating money above and beyond what they already paid in taxes for public goods. Sound crazy? We thought so too—until we saw it work. Over the years, Citizinvestor has been used to fund an eclectic collection of civic projects, from building community gardens in Philadelphia to replacing rusty bike racks on a high school campus in Oregon to erecting a statue honoring Navy veterans outside Chicago. In an age in which *taxes* is a four-letter word and cities are scoffed at for being filled with crime, pollution, poverty, and run-down public spaces, what would motivate so many citizens to donate substantial sums of money to public projects? Deep down, I think we know we were created to help restore the brokenness of cities and to use our creativity to build better public spaces. We have a sense that the brokenness we see in cities is not God's intent—that the city was meant to be made whole and perfect.

As Christians, we know where this heart for cities stems from: it stems from God's design for us to spend eternity with him in the perfect city, the New Jerusalem, which we will explore further in chapter 12. As pastor Timothy Keller points out in *Why God Made Cities*:

> Most people who read the Bible know that God invented the family. It's not a human creation. God invented it, because God reveals himself as a father, and he tells us we're children. Therefore, though sin has taken the family and often turned it into a place of abuse and pain, we don't abandon the family as an institution. We are called to redeem and rebuild the family. Do you see the pattern? The human family is a pattern given by God. Therefore, we believe it was good once and will be good again. We know the future of humanity is, in some respects, a family. God is also building a city. He is a city architect, an urban planner, and we are citizens of that city. . . . If sin has twisted the city as it's twisted the family, and

turned it into a place of pain and suffering just as it's done to the family, that doesn't mean we get rid of the city. We don't scoff at it or take pleasure in its troubles. We as Christians are called to redeem and rebuild the city. Do you see the logic? God invented the city, so we don't abandon it—we build it.[9]

So while Citizinvestor's mission and the products we create are not overtly evangelical, I believe we are revealing God's character in a meaningful way, demonstrating to the world his love for cities and the people who inhabit them. It's worth noting that none of this theology was on my mind when we were starting the company. Like Lewis, my cofounders and I didn't lock ourselves in a room until we came up with an idea for a product that would reveal God's character. But through time, prayer, and communion with other Christians, the Lord graciously revealed to us how our creation might, in some small way, be used to make God known in cities around the world.

> The number of products we can create to reveal God's character are as limitless as our ability to learn more about who he is.

The number of products we can create to reveal God's character are as limitless as our ability to learn more about who he is. C. S. Lewis created products that help us understand God's redemptive plan. Citizinvestor helps reveal God's love of cities and city-dwellers. Still other entrepreneurs create to reveal different characteristics of their Creator or to love and serve others.

Create Products That Love Others

When Jesus was asked to single out the greatest of all the commandments, he replied, "'Love the Lord your God with all your heart and with all your soul and with all your mind.' This is the first and greatest commandment. And the second is like it: 'Love your neighbor as yourself'" (Matt. 22:37–39).

On the surface, the idea of loving your neighbor appears to be one that both Christian and non-Christian entrepreneurs can agree upon. Entrepreneurs learn quickly that unless they serve the needs of customers in the marketplace, their business will fail. But Christians should be marked by a higher standard for what it means to love and serve others. For example, a non-Christian entrepreneur might see opening a strip club as a way of serving others. If customers show up and pay, the entrepreneur could claim that they are clearly serving the market as evidenced by demand for the product. Christians have a different definition of love and service though, as we worship the Author and perfect manifestation of true love. Paul most famously defined Christian love in 1 Corinthians 13:4–7:

> Love is patient, love is kind. It does not envy, it does not boast, it is not proud. It does not dishonor others, it is not self-seeking, it is not easily angered, it keeps no record of wrongs. Love does not delight in evil but rejoices with the truth. It always protects, always trusts, always hopes, always perseveres.

The bar for loving others couldn't be higher. For those of us who are called to create, this genuine love will significantly influence the products we choose to create to love and serve others.

For ten years, Scott Harrison's job as a club promoter was to get people drunk and make them believe they were living the high life. In the eyes of the world, Harrison was loving his neighbors by serving a need in the market. "I spent about a decade in New York City chasing the fast life as a nightclub promoter—basically throwing fashion and music parties for a living," Harrison recalled. "I had moved to NYC to rebel against a conservative Christian upbringing, and did that with relish, living selfishly and arrogantly."[10]

Harrison's entrepreneurial skills led to a lot of success as a club promoter, but ultimately the nightlife scene led to the unraveling of his life. At the bottom of the pit, Harrison remembers thinking, "I'm doing massive amounts of drugs, I've got a gambling problem, I smoke two packs a day, I drink every day, I'm addicted to pornography, I hang out in strip clubs. I'm a mess."[11] In retrospect, he said:

I was the worst person I knew. I'd walked away from all the spirituality and morality I'd embraced as a child, and felt completely bankrupt. I got people wasted for a living in nightclubs, and effectively the drunker they got, the more money I made. I started reading a book by A. W. Tozer called *The Pursuit of God*, and it just really rocked me. Here was an author trying to serve God desperately, living a life of submission and a life of service, and my life looked exactly opposite. Everything was about me.[12]

Harrison added, "Faced with spiritual bankruptcy, I wanted desperately to revive a lost Christian faith with action."[13] Sitting in a nightclub at five in the morning at the age of twenty-eight, Harrison decided to make a change.[14] "I offered my life to God in service, and that led me quickly out of nightclubs, and to Liberia for a new journey."[15] That journey began with Harrison volunteering as a photojournalist onboard Mercy Ship, a floating hospital that offered free medical care in the world's poorest nations. It wasn't long after hopping off the ship in Liberia that Harrison's heart really started to change.

> I fell in love with Liberia—a country with no public electricity, running water or sewage. Spending time in a leper colony and many remote villages, I put a face to the world's 1.2 billion living in poverty. Those living on less than $365 a year—money I used to blow on a bottle of Grey Goose vodka at a fancy club. Before tip.[16]

While in Liberia, Harrison began to develop an idea for a product he could create that would genuinely love others. "I said, 'Before I die, I've probably got forty-five years to throw at this. What if I could end the water crisis? What if I could see a day where every man, woman and child had clean water to drink?'"[17]

Once back in the United States, Harrison threw himself a thirty-first birthday party that looked significantly different from the parties of his twenties. Instead of receiving gifts, he charged his friends twenty dollars each to attend the party. But instead of the money going toward a cover charge for alcohol, Harrison donated the fifteen thousand dollars he raised that night to fix three water wells and build three new ones at a refugee camp in Northern Uganda.[18] This was the birth of Charity: Water, a nonprofit founded by Harrison that provides clean and safe drinking water to people in developing nations. Since its founding in 2006, Charity: Water has funded more than 22,936 water projects in twenty-four countries, but their mission is not complete. Harrison and his team's audacious mission is to "[bring] clean and safe drinking water to people in developing countries."[19]

One of the things that makes Charity: Water so unique is how they raise money, tapping into the social networks of people who donate their birthdays and social capital to raise money from friends. These are the same skills that made Harrison a successful club promoter. "My background was ten years of getting people drunk in nightclubs," he said.

> This was before Twitter. We basically emailed and called people, and tried to create an illusion that their lives were meaningful if they came, spent money, and spent time on the other side of our velvet rope. We told stories about who was there, and tried to get people jealous of what they'd missed out on if they hadn't been there. After my transformation, I tried to redeem some of the things I learned during my decade of nightlife. And as I was always an early adopter: Facebook, Twitter, Instagram, they just became part of our communication language. They seemed like great ways to bring people together, and most importantly, tell stories. The stories were all just different this time: Meaningful.[20]

Reimagining his life as service to the One who called him to create changed what it meant for Harrison to love others as himself. Today, instead of selling alcohol, he sells clean water for the world. Harrison's prodigal-son-in-the-pigsty moment didn't cause him to ignore and neglect the entrepreneurial gifts that made him such a successful club promoter. But it did drastically change what he created. For entrepreneurs who have been called to create, the gospel transforms everything we do, including what we make.

While Harrison used alcohol in his younger years as a means of destroying the lives of his neighbors, is it possible for a follower of Christ to use alcohol to create a product that genuinely loves others? The story of Arthur Guinness shows us that it is.

Much like the people that Charity: Water serves today, Guinness's neighbors in eighteenth-century Europe were dying due to a lack of clean water. At that time, no one understood how disease was spread. People routinely drank from the same water in which they dumped their garbage and sewage, often dying as a result. This led many Europeans to avoid water altogether. Instead they drank alcohol, and for good reason. The process of making alcoholic beverages killed the germs in water that led to disease. But soon excessive drinking set in, leading to what historians have deemed "the Gin Craze." Drunkenness became a major problem, leading to an increase in crime and poverty. Like everything under the sun, eighteenth-century Europeans twisted a good thing into a product that harmed rather than loved people. This was the world Guinness was born into.

> For entrepreneurs who have been called to create, the gospel transforms everything we do, including what we make.

A devout Christian, Arthur Guinness saw something in creation that he knew how to redeem to better love his neighbors. Guinness knew that beer could be part of the solution to Europe's problems of drunkenness and disease. As Guinness's biographer Stephen Mansfield points out:

> [Beer] was lower in alcohol, it was safe . . . and it was nutritious in ways scientists are only now beginning to understand. Monks brewed it, evangelicals brewed it and aspiring young entrepreneurs like Guinness brewed it. And they were respected and honored for their good works.[21]

Guinness saw an opportunity to create a product that would genuinely love and serve others. And the Lord used him in incredible ways to love people through the products he created and the company he built. Guinness beer—delicious, nutritious, filling, safe, and relatively low in alcohol—became a favorite of the people of Ireland and the brewery's growth exploded. The rest is history well known and well drunk. Guinness's integration of his faith and his work as an entrepreneur led him to be on the lookout for where God was moving in his day and age. As Mansfield points out:

> Harry Grattan Guinness [Arthur's grandson] had a favorite saying . . . borrowed from . . . Prince Albert: "Gentlemen, find out the will of God for your day and generation, and then, as quickly as possible, get into line." There is little question that much of the Guinness success and . . . impact on society came from living in light of this maxim of conduct.
>
> It is not hard to imagine Arthur Guinness wondering . . . what his role in this life might be. He would consider his abilities . . . and think deeply about what brought him pride and joy. In time, he would recognize his skills as a brewer and make it his life's work. . . .
>
> We are used to preachers and to great noisy works for God. We are used to religion that is sometimes an escape from daily life and to faith as fixation on life in another world. What Arthur Guinness founded was a venture propelled by faith, yes—but by a kind of faith that inspires men to make their work in this world an offering to God, to understand craft and discipline, love of labor and skills transferred from father to son as sacred things. It was a venture of faith that took the fruit of the earth and, through study and strain, made of it something of greater value.[22]

God cares deeply about what we create. As these stories show, entrepreneurs are empowered to create products that reveal his character and love others. Where is God moving in your cultural context today? Where do you see an opportunity to create a product that will make him better known through the revelation of his character or service to humankind? The number of products we can create in line with these objectives is only limited by our creativity and our attunement to the Lord's movement around us. "Find out the will of God for your day and generation," be on the lookout for where the true Aslan is moving, and use your God-given abilities to create products that join him in his work.

6

how we create

A teenage girl walks through the mall, swinging a bright yellow bag on her arm. In it is a pair of jeans, a tube top, and a T-shirt she just purchased, all for less than twenty dollars. On the bottom of the bag is something even more surprising than the insanely low prices: "John 3:16." The bag is from retail mammoth Forever 21, which has famously printed the Bible verse on their iconic yellow bags all around the world.

Forever 21's founders are well-known for their Christian faith. They "attend church daily, give generously to their church, and attend mission trips."[1] But the company maintains that "The faith of the founders is separate to [sic] the brand—the bag is simply a statement of faith."[2]

The company is right that there does seem to be a separation between the faith of the founders and the business they run. For starters, the Forever 21 brand is built around selling less-than-modest clothing to teenage girls. But the disconnect doesn't stop with the products Forever 21 chooses to make. What's perhaps more out of step with the founders' faith is how their business operates. A Google search for how Forever 21 is able to sell clothes so cheaply yields no shortage of reports of workers being denied pay and working in sweatshop-like conditions. Over the years, the company has been hit with numerous lawsuits charging them with violating labor laws.[3] They've also been sued more than fifty times for copyright infringement, allegedly stealing the designs of other fashion designers.[4]

Somewhere there's a disconnect. Forever 21's founders seem to be quite religious. But from the outside looking in, it doesn't appear as if their faith has been integrated holistically into their business, impacting every crevice of how the business is run.

Contrast Forever 21 with another Southern California brand that also prints John 3:16 and other Bible verses on the bottom of their products: In-N-Out Burger. As Dave Blanchard and the team at Praxis point out in their excellent book *From Concept to Scale*, "[In-N-Out Burger is] known for printing Bible references in small letters underneath its milkshake cups and on hamburger wrappers, a fairly innocuous statement of faith. But without substance backing the Bible verses, the words wouldn't be worth the negligible cost of the additional ink. What truly differentiates In-N-Out is the set of choices the company has made on the most meaningful issues."[5]

In 1948, In-N-Out's founder, Harry Snyder, wrote a simple mission statement for the company that remains unchanged today: "Serve only the highest quality product, prepare it in a clean and sparkling environment, and serve it in a warm and friendly manner."[6] The Snyder family's eventual inclusion of

Bible verses on their packaging was a reflection of a faith that had already been deeply integrated into the business in two primary ways: striving for excellence in everything and prioritizing people over profit.

The first time I tried In-N-Out was when I was visiting a friend from college who was spending the summer interning in Hollywood. She had only lived in California for a few months but she was already a raving fan of the fast-food chain and insisted I try it. Before I even tasted the food, I could sense that In-N-Out was different. The staff seemed happy to be at work. The store was clean. The service was excellent. And the place was jam-packed with giddy, loyal customers using secret code words like "animal style" to order things I didn't see on the menu. Then I tasted the difference. Even as a college student used to ravaging my body with horrible ingredients, I could tell that this burger was different from anything I'd had at any other fast-food hamburger chain. The ingredients were fresher, higher quality, and tastier. The yellow neon sign behind the counter, which read "Quality You Can Taste," was not just a slogan. Everything about In-N-Out was truly excellent.

As I have learned more about In-N-Out over the years, it has become clear why their employees always seem so happy to be at work. In-N-Out truly prioritizes people over profit. As Stacy Perman points out in her biography of the company:

> From the start, In-N-Out paid its employees more than the going rate (associates always made at least two to three dollars above minimum wage) and was an early practitioner of profit sharing. Under Rich [Snyder, the second generation operator of the business], In-N-Out went further, establishing an expansive set of benefits under which part-time workers

received free meals, paid vacations, 401(k) plans, and flexible schedules. Full-time associates also received medical, dental, vision, life and travel insurance.[7]

Not only does the company provide its employees with superior compensation and benefits but it also gives them real opportunity to advance within the company. "In-N-Out's store managers (about eighty percent of whom began at the very bottom, picking up trash, before moving up through the ranks) earned salaries equal to if not greater than most college graduates." By 2010, store managers were earning at least one hundred thousand dollars annually.[8]

Yes, the founders of In-N-Out Burger have a history of being overtly evangelical, sponsoring radio broadcasts that present the gospel, holding prayer meetings with staff in their homes, and, of course, including Bible verses on their packaging. But these outward expressions of the founders' faith are backed up by a business that demonstrates an understanding of the gospel in many other areas of the company.

For those who are called to create, our faith should impact every aspect of our entrepreneurial endeavors, from our motivations for creating to the products we choose to create to how we operate our ventures. God is always on the move in the world around us. The entrepreneur who is attuned to God's Word and his Spirit will continually find ways to use their ventures to carry out his will. Too often, Christian entrepreneurs start a venture without thinking deeply about how their faith should impact the entirety of their organization. Instead, they make all of the Ts in their logo crosses, slap a Bible verse on their packaging, or sponsor a Little League team. These are not bad things but they are largely meaningless if they are not accompanied by a deeper and more holistic integration of the gospel throughout the organization.

When my father was starting up his now-successful food distribution business, he wanted to craft a mission statement that made the connection between his faith and work explicitly clear to the world. And so, for the past fifteen years, his employees have driven hundreds of thousands of miles across central Florida with the following statement plastered on the back of their trucks: "Our mission is to fulfill the specific needs of each customer by offering quality product, exceptional customer service, and exemplifying Jesus Christ in every facet of business and life." Over the years, my father's customers, vendors, employees, and even strangers who share the road with his drivers have been made aware of why his company exists. But that mission statement would be useless—and, in fact, terribly detrimental—if my father didn't "exemplify Jesus Christ" with actions that backed up those words. My father is known in the community as a follower of Jesus Christ not because of his company's mission statement but because he is exceedingly generous, winsome, and hospitable to "the least of these." In short, my father has holistically integrated the gospel throughout his business.

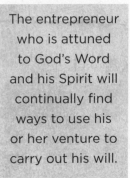

The entrepreneur who is attuned to God's Word and his Spirit will continually find ways to use his or her venture to carry out his will.

The gospel has the power to change everything, including how we create. As In-N-Out Burger and other similar organizations show us, two of the best ways we can more deeply integrate our faith into how our businesses operate are striving for excellence in everything we do and prioritizing people over profit.

Excellence in Everything

Throughout Scripture, Christians are commanded to do everything with excellence, not doing anything halfheartedly. Why? Because when God creates he does it with excellence, and as his image-bearers to the world we should seek to imitate Him in every way possible. Jesus again provides the perfect model here. Jesus came to earth as God's ultimate image-bearer, and as we've seen, he spent his working days emulating the entrepreneurial and creative character of his Father. Have you ever stopped to think about *how* Jesus would have created? As Dorothy Sayers imagines:

> No crooked table legs or ill-fitting drawers ever, I dare swear, came out of the carpenter's shop at Nazareth. Nor, if they did, could anyone believe that they were made by the same hand that made Heaven and earth. No piety in the worker will compensate for work that is not true to itself; for any work that is untrue to its own technique is a living lie.[9]

For our work to reflect the First Entrepreneur, we must strive for excellence in everything we do. In the words of Reverend Robert Sirico, "Searching for excellence is the beginning of a search for God."[10]

> If our work is to be a reflection of the First Entrepreneur, we must strive for excellence in everything we do.

Perhaps no company demonstrates excellence as well as Chick-fil-A. From their incredibly consistent food to their top-notch team members, Chick-fil-A clearly operates with a higher commitment to excellence than most businesses today, and

104

this stems largely from the Christian faith of the company's founder, Truett Cathy.

In the mid-1990s, Chick-fil-A was facing its first real threat in the "quick-service" chicken market from a startup chain called Boston Chicken, which would later be renamed Boston Market. Founded in 1995, Boston Market grew fast, and the company had plans to grow even faster to reach one billion dollars in sales by the year 2000, a sales number Chick-fil-A hadn't hit in all its fifty years in business.

This aggressive competitor had Chick-fil-A executives nervous, so much so that the team began focusing on how the company could grow bigger and faster to keep up. These conversations culminated in a boardroom meeting at Chick-fil-A's headquarters in Atlanta, Georgia, with executives lining both sides of the table, going back and forth about how the company could outgrow Boston Market. All through the meeting, Chick-fil-A's founder, Truett Cathy, sat quietly at the end of the table, seemingly disengaged from the boardroom banter. Then, all of a sudden, Cathy uncharacteristically banged his fist on the table and all eyes turned to him. "I am sick and tired of hearing you talk about us getting bigger," he said. "What we need to be talking about is getting better! If we get better, our customers will demand that we get bigger."[11]

The outburst shifted the focus of the meeting and the rest of the decade for Chick-fil-A. Poetically, Boston Market filed for bankruptcy while Chick-fil-A hit one billion dollars in sales for the first time in 2000.

In a culture that tells businesses to prioritize growth over quality, Chick-fil-A consistently swims upstream, striving first for excellence in everything they do. For example, in 2014 the company rolled out an excellent new line of grilled

chicken products. But unlike other fast-food chains that seemingly introduce new products every other week, Chick-fil-A
invested *seven years* into testing more than twelve hundred
recipes to ensure the products were "remarkable."[12]

Chick-fil-A does nothing quickly. But they do almost everything with excellence. This commitment to quality is baked
into everything they do, including the company's name. As
Truett Cathy explained in his autobiography, *Eat Mor Chikin:
Inspire More People*, the capitalization of the letter "A" in
Chick-fil-A's name stands "for top quality." Today, on the
walls of many Chick-fil-As, you will read the words of the
company's now-deceased founder: "Food is essential to life.
Therefore, make it good."

Truett Cathy lived a life that reflected Jesus Christ, from
his and his wife's care of the fatherless to their teaching of
Sunday school to their genuine care of people. But the way
Cathy operated Chick-fil-A, striving for excellence in everything the company does, will likely be one of the greatest
testaments to his understanding that he was created to reflect
the image of his Caller.

As Cathy was approaching his eightieth birthday, his children, all of whom were involved in the operations of Chick-fil-A
at the time, invited their mother and father to meet them for
dinner at Chick-fil-A's headquarters. There they presented their
parents with a covenant to continue to operate the company in a
way both their earthly and heavenly fathers would be proud of:

> We will be faithful to Christ's lordship in our lives. As com-
> mitted Christians we will live a life of selfless devotion to His
> calling in our lives. . . . We will be faithful to carry on our
> family and corporate heritage . . . we commit to operating

Chick-fil-A restaurants with standards of excellence in our products, service, and cleanliness.[13]

Chick-fil-A's commitment to quality is more than just a good business strategy; it's rooted in an understanding that the creation and further development of Chick-fil-A is a "calling" from God to reflect his character of excellence.

People over Profit

In the past ten years, it would be difficult to find entrepreneurs more celebrated and praised than Steve Jobs (founder of Apple) and Elon Musk (founder of Tesla and SpaceX). While these two are certainly famous for their success in business, they are also infamously known for how poorly they treat the people around them. As a former employee said of Musk:

> Elon's worst trait by far, in my opinion, is a complete lack of loyalty or human connection. Many of us worked tirelessly for him for years and were tossed to the curb like a piece of litter without a second thought. What was clear is that people who worked for him were like ammunition: used for a specific purpose until exhausted and discarded.[14]

There is perhaps no clearer way for Christians to set themselves apart from the world than by prioritizing people over profit.

The celebration of entrepreneurs like Jobs and Musk in movies, books, and endless magazine covers has created a caricature of the ideal entrepreneur that prioritizes product, process, and profit over people. In this line of thinking, people are meaningless—interchangeable parts, there only to maximize productivity or else be "discarded." Against this backdrop, there is perhaps no clearer way for Christians to set themselves apart from the world than by prioritizing people over profit and everything else. In the same sermon referenced in chapter 1 of this book, Pastor Jerry King put it this way:

> Do not forget that in God's Kingdom, it's people—redeemed lives—that are His masterpieces. That's what He's about, through the whole sweep of His history. It's redeemed lives that God calls His treasure. So in the predictable clashes of people and product, people win every time. Let the stuff go. It doesn't matter, not comparatively. It's people.[15]

Contrast Musk's style of firing people with that of Sevenly, the social good venture that designs and sells "cause art" in the form of T-shirts and other products to raise money for a different nonprofit every seven days. In his book *People Over Profit*, the company's Christian founder, Dale Partridge, hammers home this message that "people matter," heeding Jesus's call to "love your neighbor as yourself," even when you are firing someone.

> Termination doesn't mean [someone is] a bad person or [is] worthless. It just means that they may not work well here at this current moment. It's just as unfair for the employee as it is for us to keep them in their current position when we know it doesn't work. Yet . . . termination can still be a devastating process. So at Sevenly, we have a unique twist on the golden rule: fire others the way you would want to be fired. When we explain our reasoning, we never discuss personal flaws; we always talk about the work. We try to provide them with a generous severance regardless of their tenure, and don't penny pinch. Why? Because we know they

are people with spouses and kids and houses. . . . If at all possible, we write them a letter of recommendation extolling their positive traits. . . . We have the team go around and affirm them by sharing what they love about them and we even pray over them. People who transition out are not fired employees; we consider them alumni. Our goal is that when a former team member leaves our company they'll say, "It didn't work out for me at Sevenly in the end, but they are a darn good company."[16]

In 2002, Bob Collins had one of the most powerful jobs in finance and was responsible for investing thirty-six billion dollars of assets for Goldman Sachs's clients as the firm's managing director and co-chief investment officer in London. Today he owns a chain of laundromats. No, this is not the fictional plot of *Trading Places 2*. This is the story of how one Christian entrepreneur followed God's call to change the way certain businesses are run, prioritizing people over profit.

"In many ways, I could not have imagined a more fun and rewarding position than the one I had at Goldman," Collins said to me. "When you are a manager for thirty-six billion dollars in investments, you're basically treated like someone who is personally worth thirty-six billion dollars. I could get a meeting with anyone I wanted. I could literally just pick up the phone and call the CEO of Coca-Cola, Cisco, or whichever company I wanted and they would take my call." Collins had a tremendous platform that was about to grow even larger with the prospect of making partner at Goldman on the horizon, a position that would have netted him between six and eight million dollars annually.

But while Collins loved his job, he was beginning to see the toll it was taking on his life. "Spiritually, Goldman was a very unhealthy environment," he shares. "I was a pretty crappy husband. I was a pretty crappy father. At the time, we had five kids between the ages of five and twelve and I was always traveling. I didn't like myself and I knew the source of that was the toxic environment I was in." So, at the age of thirty-seven, Collins decided to retire and walk away from a career almost nobody walks away from. "It was like I was playing outfield for the New York Yankees and then, in the prime of my career, I decided to hang up my cleats. People thought I was crazy."

Collins left the posh cobblestone streets of London and moved his family back home to Florida, where he worked to discern where God was calling him to serve in the next chapter of his life. The Lord eventually led Collins to start a Tampa-based chapter of the National Christian Foundation, where, since 2004, Collins and team have facilitated more than $260 million in giving. In his role at the foundation, Collins has had the opportunity to work with countless Christian entrepreneurs, helping them donate some of the profits from their businesses to kingdom-building causes. As he explains, "I was working with and serving all of these Christian business owners, and I was seeing how they were operating their businesses differently from the rest of the world, and I was like, 'This is amazing!'" Collins was seeing a model for holistically integrating the gospel into businesses, letting it impact every crevice of the organization. At some point he thought, *Well, I can do this.*

Collins began to catch a vision for his next venture, Grace Harbor Group, which would acquire businesses that traditionally do not prioritize people over profit (especially the poor) and work to turn around the way they operated. "That's when I felt called to go into the laundromat business," he said. It wasn't immediately clear to me how laundromats mistreat the poor, but Collins's partner, Andrew Prilliman, helped me understand. "In the laundromat industry, the mantra is 'Get them in, get them out, and get their money,'" Prilliman said. Often owned by absentee investors who see the stores purely as ATMs, laundromats, like many businesses in the poorest areas of town, don't need to prioritize people over profit because their customers don't have the freedom to choose where to take their business. Laundromat customers often have trouble finding reliable transportation and are thus forced to use the closest coin laundry service, even if that store is poorly lit, unsafe, and degrading. As Prilliman shares, "We know laundromat owners who don't run the air conditioning, who refuse to play music or spend money on TVs. In their minds, the laundromat is not a place to hang out."

But the gospel gave Collins, Prilliman, and the team at Grace Harbor a different perspective on the laundromat business. Rather than viewing people as mere units of profit to get in and out the door as quickly as possible, the Grace Harbor team saw a rare opportunity to love and serve some of the poorest members of society. "There are not that many businesses where you get to have meaningful, ongoing interactions with the poor," Collins said. "Here's an industry where you have people sitting around for hours at a time," Prilliman added. "You have a captive audience, typically made up of the less fortunate of society. What a great opportunity to serve the very people Jesus called us to love and care for. What a great opportunity to build relationships and community."

As I walked into one of the laundromats Grace Harbor had recently acquired and renovated, it was immediately clear to me that this was a place designed for people to come and stay comfortably. The store was well lit, freshly painted, and clean. It felt more like a community center than a laundromat, with free Wi-Fi, TVs, and even the opportunity to pick up a Cuban sandwich. It felt like a business that treated people like, well, people.

But the clearest sign that this laundromat was different were the smiles on customers' faces. Prilliman credits the laundromat's managers for the store's happy customers, saying, "Our managers' job is to remember people's names and really get to know them, because we want this store to feel like a family." After acquiring their first four laundromats in 2015, the Grace Harbor team began searching for store managers who could run a solid business but who would also continually prioritize people over profit. They were looking for people who, because of their understanding of the gospel of Jesus Christ, demonstrated a genuine love for people. This led Prilliman and team to make hiring decisions that bucked conventional business wisdom. "Some of our managers have records. Some have been homeless. Out of all the candidates out there, they would typically not be the top picks to manage these stores." But, as Prilliman and team have learned, these are often the people who understand and live out the gospel best.

Bill and Diane, the husband-and-wife management team of the laundromat I visited, are a great example. Before being hired to manage the laundromat, Bill and Diane had been unemployed, struggling to make ends meet. Now, with the opportunity given to them by Grace Harbor, Bill and Diane are meeting the needs of others. "I've always had a big heart for people," Diane said. She then told me a story of a regular customer who had just delivered a baby when the father died unexpectedly. "I told her, 'If there's anything I can do to help you—if I can buy you diapers, or if you need to wash clothes and you don't have the means—come to me. I'll help you out. I'll wash you a load.'" Because Diane genuinely cared for this woman and took the time to get to know her rather than viewing her as just another faceless customer, she was able to take advantage of an opportunity to demonstrate the love of Christ.

While Bill and Diane are investing in the lives of their customers, the Grace Harbor team is investing in them. As Prilliman explained, "We are entrepreneurs who believe in the biblical call to create. We want to empower others to fulfill that same calling. We take managers like Bill and Diane, who we know will represent Jesus Christ well in their own business, and say, 'Let us help you create your own business, running a Wash/Dry/Fold service on our platform at the laundromat. We have the store, we have the machines, we pay the rent, we pay the electric bill. But we want to help you own your own business. Your success will help our own business, because the more Wash/Dry/Fold services you sell, the more quarters you are sticking into our machines.'" Prilliman and team have helped Bill and Diane and other managers navigate every step of the process of launching and growing their own businesses, from setting up LLCs to securing business checking accounts to coaching the new entrepreneurs on how to sell the Wash/Dry/Fold service to corporate accounts.

On the surface, it doesn't make a lot of sense for Grace Harbor to hire inexperienced people to manage their laundromats. It makes even less sense to spend time and capital training them on how to run their own business. But the gospel is constantly challenging us to think contrarily about the wisdom of the world, opening our eyes to new opportunities to carry out God's will. The team at Grace Harbor understands this and has thought deeply about how the gospel should influence the operations of their businesses.

"I think the perception is that a Christian business owner is a person who runs their business like everybody else but they go to church on Sundays and they have a fish in their logo. That's the only difference," Prilliman said. "I got connected with another Christian laundromat owner who took me to visit one of his locations. I walked in and almost fell over because there was this huge mural of Jesus and a lamb and little kids running around him. I went back to our office and said, 'That's the picture of what we *don't* want to be.' I want people to feel loved when they are at our stores. I want them to feel like we care. I want them to feel like we value who they are. We don't have to prove to people that we are Christians through their senses. We want to appeal to people's hearts."

For those of us who are called to create, we are never done thinking about how the priorities of our Caller impact the why, what, and how of our creating. Maybe God is showing you opportunities to demonstrate excellence in everything your business does, maybe he is showing you innovative ways of prioritizing people over profit, or maybe he is showing you something else entirely. It is up to you to do the work of communing with your Caller regularly to discern where he is calling you to act next.

As we do that work, we will be faced with challenges that are unique or especially acute because we have chosen to create for the One who has called us rather than for ourselves. It is those challenges that we will focus on in part 3 of this book.

PART 3

challenges

7

trust, hustle, and rest

Ai Ching Goh came to faith in Christ after founding the Malaysian-based company she runs today as cofounder and CEO. This has given Goh an interesting perspective on entrepreneurship, seeing her company through two very different lenses. Goh, who grew up in a Taoist family in Malaysia, has always been an overachiever. "I always needed to be the best at everything I did," she said. "I always needed to prove a point to my dad, the father of four daughters. I've always shouldered the responsibility and burden of wanting to be 'the only son,' which is a big deal in the Asian context." Part of Goh assuming the role of the only son was choosing a career path that began at Procter & Gamble and has culminated thus far in her founding of PikToChart, a web-based, do-it-yourself infographic maker that has grown to more than five million users in just four years.[1] Goh was living a life any parent would be proud of. "I got good grades, I had a good career, I found a husband relatively early in life," she says.

"But it was on my wedding day that everything crumbled and fell apart."

After walking down the aisle, Goh realized she had neglected to finalize some travel arrangements for her and her husband's honeymoon. The trip was off, and Goh began to unravel. "I melted down. I was very, very, *very* tired at that point. I was running PikToChart, I was planning our wedding. Once the honeymoon fell through, I essentially fell apart." Goh had been "hustling"—startup culture's favorite word to describe the extreme work ethic often necessary to help new ventures succeed. Like most entrepreneurs, Goh discovered that an overemphasis on hustling can lead to crushing expectations and burnout. "Prior to my conversion to Christianity, I hustled constantly," Goh says. "I was always going a hundred miles an hour, I was frequently ill, I was agitated and temperamental, and I couldn't sleep because my mind was always on the business. I was married to my job. I was a workaholic."

After her post-wedding meltdown, Goh was invited by a Christian friend to take a break to visit her in Korea. It was during this time of relative rest that Goh began to sense God pursuing her. Goh surrendered her life to Christ and, with the help of her friend, began attending a local church back home in Malaysia, at the risk of being persecuted by her family. Within two months, Goh had read the Bible from cover to cover and she began to see that her workaholism was really a means of trying to save herself. In Christ, Goh found rest; and while God had clearly called Goh to create, using her considerable skills to serve him and others, her eyes were opened to what Scripture makes clear: that it is God, not us, who produces results; and that in order to find true rest hustling must be accompanied by even greater trusting in God.

"I used to think I was in control, that if I followed a specific formula I would be successful," Goh said. "But once I realized God was in control, it felt like a load of worries had been lifted from my shoulders. I realized everything was in his hands and I had far less control than I thought." Even when Goh knew these truths intellectually, it took a disciplined prayer life and time in God's Word for her to maintain this perspective. "For me, this is a lifelong process. My flesh wants to rely on my hustle. But prayer and time in Scripture reminds me that it is God, not me, who produces success through my endeavors," she said. "The busier I get, the more time I spend in prayer. I make it a point to start my day at 6:00 a.m. with prayer, and that has given me a tremendous amount of rest. It's essential for me to constantly seek a bigger perspective on God and remind myself that he is in control of everything. When I forget that, I feel like I have to be in control. Prayer helps me understand that everything is in his hands and I can be still and know that he is God. There are times when he calls us to hustle and there are times when he calls us to be still and watch him do the work."

> It is God, not us, who produces results. In order to find true rest, hustling must be accompanied by even greater trusting in God.

One of Goh's favorite verses is Joshua 24:13, in which God reminds the Israelites that it was he alone who was responsible for bringing them into the Promised Land: "I gave you a land on which you did not toil and cities you did not build; and you live in them and eat from vineyards and olive groves that you did not plant." Goh uses this verse to

remind herself that while God calls us to work hard and
hustle, he is more interested in seeing us trust and rely on
him, even when we look ridiculous to the rest of the world
in the process.

An earlier passage in the book of Joshua provides an excellent case study on this tension between trusting and hustling.
While the Israelites were being led by Joshua to the Promised Land, they came upon a major impasse: Jericho, a city
fortified by a double ring of walls providing its citizens with
eighteen feet of protection from would-be attackers. To make
matters worse, Jericho was built on a hill, requiring attackers to lay siege to the city at a steep incline. In other words,
the city was nearly impossible to penetrate. But as Joshua
6:2 records, "The Lord said to Joshua, 'See, I have delivered
Jericho into your hands.'" Instead of giving Joshua and the
Israelites superhuman strength and agility so they could take
Jericho on their own, though, God required them to place
an inordinate amount of trust in him. He instructed Joshua:

> March around the city once with all the armed men. Do
> this for six days. Have seven priests carry trumpets of rams'
> horns in front of the ark. On the seventh day, march around
> the city seven times, with the priests blowing the trumpets.
> When you hear them sound a long blast on the trumpets,
> have the whole army give a loud shout; then the wall of the
> city will collapse and the army will go up, everyone straight
> in. (vv. 3–5)

Like so many other times in history, God chose to use "the
foolish things of the world to shame the wise" (1 Cor. 1:27).
Rather than allowing Joshua and the Israelites to win the
battle in their own strength, God laid out a plan to ensure

that he alone would get the glory. Before giving the Israelites victory, God asked them to trust him to provide. Without blinking, Joshua did just that. The very next verse tells us that Joshua turned to the Israelites and gave them God's marching orders verbatim. The Israelites trusted in God's plan. Then they hustled: marching, blowing their trumpets, and shouting until Jericho's walls collapsed.

Of course, it wasn't the Israelites' marching, shouting, and hustling that brought the walls of Jericho tumbling down. It was God. And that's exactly what I think God wanted the Israelites—and us—to see. As entrepreneurs, we know how to hustle, how to work hard, how to earn our sweat equity. And that is a good thing! Colossians 3:23 commands us to "work . . . with all your heart, as working for the Lord." But believing that our hustle is what is responsible for producing results in our ventures would be like the Israelites believing that shouting brought an impenetrable fortress crumbling to the ground. All throughout Scripture, God reminds us of who deserves the credit for producing success and wealth:

> You may say to yourself, "My power and the strength of my hands have produced this wealth for me." But remember the LORD your God, for it is he who gives you the ability to produce wealth. (Deut. 8:17–18)

> Wealth and honor come from you;
>   you are the ruler of all things.
> In your hands are strength and power
>   to exalt and give strength to all. (1 Chron. 29:12)

Remain in me, as I also remain in you. No branch can bear fruit by itself; it must remain in the vine. Neither can you bear fruit unless you remain in me. I am the vine; you are

123

the branches. If you remain in me and I in you, you will bear much fruit; apart from me you can do nothing. (John 15:4–5)

Those of us who are called to create are forced to wrestle with the tension between trusting and hustling. On the one hand we know that apart from God we can do nothing, but on the other hand we know that God commands us to work hard. For most entrepreneurs, the hustling comes easily. It's the trusting that is so difficult. Why is it so critical that we manage this tension well? Because at the end of the day, when we rely on our hustling without trusting in God, we are either trying to play God or steal his glory, either of which leads to restlessness. So how should we think about the tension between trusting and hustling? As Joshua and the Israelites show us, we shouldn't seek to resolve the tension; instead, we should embrace it by both trusting *and* hustling. These ideas aren't in conflict with one another; they are meant to be married together.

But as Solomon shares in Proverbs 16, there is a sequence to trusting and hustling that honors the Lord and brings us great rest. In Proverbs 16:3, the wisest man who ever lived commands: "Commit to the LORD whatever you do, and he will establish your plans." So before we hustle, we are to commit our work to the Lord. This is an act of trust, recognizing that it is God alone who produces results. Next, in verse 9, Solomon urges us to hustle: "In their hearts humans plan their course, but the LORD establishes their steps." Yes, God has called us to trust in him, but he has also graciously given us minds

> When we rely on our hustling without trusting in God, we are either trying to play God or steal his glory.

124

to plan and execute. Once we have committed our works to the Lord, we are called to hustle. This is the time to design, wireframe, develop, paint, innovate, write, advertise, and sell. Finally, in the closing verse of the proverb, Solomon writes: "The lot is cast into the lap, but its every decision is from the LORD" (v. 33). If we have trusted in the Lord to produce results, and then obediently hustled, doing our best to use our God-given talents to bring our visions to life, "the lot is cast" and we can experience true rest, knowing that we are not ultimately responsible for the results. As the five women whose stories make up this chapter show us, trusting and hustling aren't at war with each other. God has commanded us to do both in a continuous cycle of trust, hustle, and rest.

Trust

In 2009, Angela Popplewell cofounded an innovative non-profit called 100cameras, which teaches kids in marginalized communities from the Lower East Side of New York to South Sudan how to share their unique perspectives through photography. 100cameras then turns the photographs into products that are sold online, directly funding medical, educational, and lifeline supplies for the kid photographers. Like most entrepreneurs, hustling comes easily to Popplewell. But, as she has learned, when hustling is not accompanied by trusting in God, it's natural to fool ourselves into believing that we are responsible for our success, setting up expectations we will inevitably fall short of. "There can easily be this savior-like mentality that enters in without me even knowing it," Popplewell shared. "This mentality tells me that it's all on me to make 100cameras work. I have to do this. The kids we support, my staff, my mentors—they all depend on me. If change is going to happen, I have to answer the call and rise up and do it. This is what makes entrepreneurship such an emotional roller coaster. When I feel like it's all on me, I rely on my hustle, and because of that, I wear the highs way too high, and I wear the lows way too low."

I can't think of a more apt term to describe this common thinking than "savior-like mentality." When we hustle and fail to recognize God as our ultimate provider, we are essentially trying to save ourselves, trying to prove to the world that we don't need a savior, that we can accomplish anything we set our minds to in our own strength.

Nicole Baker Fulgham, another nonprofit entrepreneur, knows this struggle all too well. Growing up in a working-class neighborhood in Detroit, Fulgham had a front-row seat to the problem of education inequality. Fortunately for her, Fulgham was accepted into an "exam high school" outside of her neighborhood where one hundred percent of the kids graduated and went on to college. This opportunity put Fulgham on a path to earning a bachelor's degree from the University of Michigan and a PhD in education policy from UCLA. But the other kids in Fulgham's neighborhood weren't as fortunate. "All of my friends on my block went to the neighborhood high school, where half of the students didn't graduate," Fulgham said to me. "I remember thinking, 'Wait a minute, the kids in my neighborhood are just as smart as I am. Why isn't anyone trying to help them succeed?'"

A fire had been kindled in Fulgham to help solve the problem of education inequality in America, sparked in part by her church community. "I went to an African American church every Sunday where there was a tradition of social justice and putting your faith into action," she said. After receiving her degrees from two top schools, Fulgham knew it was time to put her faith into action, a faith that, as the title of her book suggests, is concerned with *Educating* All *God's Children*. This led Fulgham to spend the first ten years of her career at Teach for America, the mammoth nonprofit whose audacious vision is that "one day, all children in this nation will have the opportunity to attain an excellent education."[2]

"I came out of Teach for America: a really large, well-run, successful nonprofit, where it was all about the hustle," Fulgham said. "It was all about setting big goals and going after them. Those are things that I treasure and that I think we need more of in faith-based organizations. There's honor in working hard." But when Fulgham followed God's call to create with the launch of her own nonprofit, The Expectations Project, she sensed a greater need for trusting in God than ever before. "What I've had to learn at The Expectations Project is the trusting piece. Our vision is pretty audacious: to get hundreds of thousands of Christians to take up education inequality in public schools. If I thought I could accomplish that vision by myself, I would be delusional. It's really about praying that God will spark people's interest in this cause. We can have the best website, the best pitch, the best talk, but if God isn't moving in people's hearts, they're just not going to take the action we need them to take."

Not only is Fulgham learning how to surrender her long-term vision for The Expectations Project to God but the day-to-day reality of running a donor-supported nonprofit requires her to constantly verbalize her trust in the Lord to provide for her and her staff. "I'm always thinking about how much financial runway we have left as an organization. I'd love to have twelve months of runway all the time, but that's not always the case. There are nine people on our team. I've had to really let go of the fact that I am not responsible for meeting their needs and their mortgages. That's God's job. I don't say that in an arrogant way; it's just if I thought I had that much control, I'd be kidding myself. I have to constantly remind myself to trust in the fact that if this is God's work and he wants it to happen, it will come as long as we are doing the diligent work on our part. I know I have to hustle, to set ambitious goals, to schedule the right meetings. But those things make me feel like I am in control. Prayer is my way of going to the Lord and admitting I am not in control. He is. And that gives me rest."

Hustle

As the battle of Jericho showed us, God wants us to articulate our trust in him so that when he does great work through us, we can't take credit for the success. This has certainly been the experience of Hannah Brencher, the founder of More Love Letters, whom we first met in chapter 4. As I sat down with Brencher, she had just experienced the impossible things God can do through us when we are willing to trust him and hustle when he calls. As she said, "I have been working on my second book for six months now, and every time I go into proposal mode, I stall and the book changes based on my feelings, or whatever I'm thinking that day, or whatever I think the world needs."

Brencher was hustling, but she was going nowhere. That's when Brencher went to the Lord and offered up her project to him. She trusted that if it was his will for her to finish another book, he would accomplish it through her. "A week ago, I had to stop and say, 'God, I don't want this to be my book. I want this to be all completely of you, but I don't know how not to take ownership over it.' I spent a good amount of time praying and I heard God clearly saying, 'The only way for this not to be your book is for me to do something you can't take credit for.'"

Almost immediately after verbalizing her trust in God for the project, Brencher caught a vision to take the book in an entirely different direction. Then it was time for her to hustle. Within five days Brencher had written twenty thousand words. To put that in perspective, it took me ten months to write the fifty-five-thousand–word book you hold in your hands.

After Brencher first trusted and then hustled, God produced results through her that she simply cannot take credit for. "At the end of this book, I'm not going to say it came about because I sat down to write it," Brencher said. "I'm going to say, 'God did something impossible through me.' I stalled for six months, and he showed up and did something in a month's time. As Christian entrepreneurs, we should be asking God to show off so much. We should ask him for big things so he can blow our expectations out of the water and get the glory from us and those around us. God needs your discipline. He needs you to hustle just as hard as any other entrepreneur. The difference is, as Christians, we know our hustle is only part of the equation. Ultimately, it is God who will produce results through us and is thus worthy of all the glory."

Rest

As we've seen demonstrated by the amazing women in this chapter, trusting is the difficult yet simple act of recognizing that we are not in control. Once we have taken this critical first step, it is certainly right to hustle, to use our God-given talents to fulfill our call to create. But how do we know if we are both trusting *and* hustling? Hustling is easy to spot. It's found in our email inboxes, our to-do lists, and our cluttered minds. But how do we know if we are truly trusting in God rather than ourselves to produce results? Perhaps the best indicator is whether or not we are at rest.

> How do we know if we are trusting in God rather than ourselves? Perhaps the best indicator is whether or not we are at rest.

Rest is what we are all craving. It doesn't take long to realize that rest means more than simply spending time out of the office. With the lines between work and home almost totally blurred, it can seem impossible to disconnect physically and mentally from the demands of incessant productivity. Even when we are at home, we are checking email, Instagram, calendars, and so forth. We are always doing. We are restless.

How can we find the rest we all so desperately long for? St. Augustine provides the answer: "Our hearts are restless, until they can find rest in You." We will be restless until we rest in God alone. For those who are called to create, this means that while we should certainly hustle, we must first trust in God who, throughout history, has been faithful to provide for his people. If we trust in God's character and steward the talents he has given us well, we can rest knowing that the results are in his hands, that he is in control and is working everything for our good. This is the only path to true and deep rest behaviorally, mentally, and spiritually, and it begins with our submission to the God-designed art of Sabbath. In the words of pastor Timothy Keller:

We are also to think of Sabbath as an act of trust. God appointed the Sabbath to remind us that he is working and resting. To practice Sabbath is a disciplined and faithful way to remember that you are not the one who keeps the world running, who provides for your family, not even the one who keeps your work projects moving forward. Entrepreneurs find it especially difficult to believe this. They have high levels of competence and very few team members. If they don't put in the hours, things don't get done. How easy to fall prey to the temptation to believe that they alone are holding up their corner of creation![3]

Sarah Lin hasn't always practiced the art of Sabbath rest. After starting her company, EllieFunDay, Lin was hustling harder than ever and for good reason: she was building a company that employed some of the world's poorest and most marginalized people.

In 2011, Lin was on a mission trip in India with her husband, Elton, when the couple saw an opportunity to design a product that would employ those in need. On the trip, Lin met a group of women who were victims of domestic abuse and human trafficking and who just happened to know how to sew at a basic level. "We did a lot of research and came to the conclusion that what these women needed most was a consistent job that would provide a fair wage to help their families thrive," Lin said.

A skilled designer with more than a decade of experience working for big corporations and agencies in the United States, Lin began brainstorming products she could create to employ these women. "I love designing hand-crafted gifts that have meaning," Lin said. "I knew if I was going to design a product, it would have to be something dear to me. For some reason, I kept coming back to the thought of my baby blanket. Growing up, my blankie was my source of security in a cold and frightening world. It had this elephant print on it, and so I called it 'ellie fun *pei*'—*pei* meaning 'blanket' in Chinese. The name EllieFunDay is an allusion to my beloved baby blanket. My blanket was so dear to me. I carried it everywhere. There was something very comforting, very empowering about my blanket. So I dreamed about designing a baby blanket that would be a source of security and empowerment. A blanket that would provide a pathway for people out of desperate poverty. That's how EllieFunDay was born."

Once the company was launched, Lin and her husband-turned-business-partner were hustling hard. It took an early failure in the business to cause them to take a step back and begin the practice of Sabbath rest. As Lin said, "As entrepreneurs, we hustle so hard we forget to stop and rest. After an early failure at EllieFunDay, I realized that we needed to step back, rest, and listen to God so that we could reevaluate what we were doing with the business. That time of rest was so life-giving that I thought, 'Why don't we do this more often?' That's when Elton and I decided that at least once a year we were going to observe a Sabbath retreat to take time to listen to God, pray for our company, and give ourselves some spiritual whitespace."

Each year, the couple disconnects from social media, limits their access to email, and gets away to rest and spend time with each other and God. "One year we rented a tiny Airbnb in the middle of Joshua Tree National Park, and it was one of the best experiences we've had," Lin said, recalling one of these Sabbath retreats. "I really related to Moses during that trip when he went out to the desert and heard God speak. I'm usually a city girl and love the energy, but being in the desert where it is utterly silent was a deeply mystical and spiritual experience. To see the stars at night in the middle of the desert really gave me a deep sense of God's grandness that I can't really experience in the city. To just sit and wonder is a luxury, but that rest is so vital to my creative soul."

Those annual Sabbath retreats led Lin to value rest and incorporate mini Sabbath moments into her daily routine through the ancient liturgical method advocated by St. Ignatius known as *examen*. Lin explained, "Examen is simply the act of mentally walking through your day to see where God has shown up. Each evening, I think through my day and try to recognize where God was moving, where he was clearly present, where he was particularly active. When things are going really well at EllieFunDay, that process helps me recognize that it is God, not me, who is the one producing wealth and success. It reminds me that I am not in control or ultimately responsible for making this business succeed. And that gives me deep rest."

Unlike the rest of the world that focuses solely on hustling, those who are called to create can recognize the paradoxical truth that it is God, not us, who produces wealth and success. This truth frees us from the burden of feeling like it's all up to us to make our ventures succeed, support our families and employees, and produce a return for investors. And that freedom brings about the rest we all so desperately crave.

8

responding to failure

As the bagpipes blared "Amazing Grace," the congregation sat somberly waiting for the service to begin. At the end of the center aisle stood a man in a clerical collar. "My name is Father Leo," the man said in greeting. "Welcome to Startup Funeral."[1]

Following Father Leo's opening remarks, entrepreneurs from three different companies took turns stepping into the pulpit to eulogize their startups and talk candidly about why their entrepreneurial endeavors had failed. The audience of friends and fellow members of New York City's startup community sat back and listened, giving these entrepreneurs a chance to publicly grieve the loss of their companies.

What makes Startup Funeral so remarkable (besides the fact that it is a "funeral" sponsored by liquor companies) is that entrepreneurs would speak so transparently about their failures. While Silicon Valley preaches the "fail fast" mantra, encouraging entrepreneurs to view failure as a learning opportunity on the path to building a better business, the fact remains that most entrepreneurs never talk transparently about their struggles and failures. In the words of Father Leo, "Startups are afraid to talk to people about what went wrong."[2]

The inability of entrepreneurs to respond openly to failure has led to an epidemic of depression and, in the most dramatic cases, suicide. According to a study by Dr. Michael Freeman, a clinical professor at the University of California, San Francisco, thirty percent of entrepreneurs experience depression, making entrepreneurs more than four times more likely than the average American to be clinically depressed.[3]

Brad Feld, an entrepreneur, investor, and one of startup culture's leading thinkers, has been blogging openly about his depression for more than a decade in an effort to make the issue less taboo. As Feld explained, in an age of relentless self-promotion where we have the power to pick and choose which pieces of our story we want to share, there's tremendous pressure for entrepreneurs to paint a near-perfect picture of their ventures. "Against the backdrop of this rah-rah everybody's killing it, everyone's doing great language, it makes it even harder to be open about [struggles and failures]," Feld said. "We're programmed and told over and over again that as leaders we have to be strong, we have to show no weakness. That tone and that dynamic is incredibly hard to deal with, especially against the backdrop of huge amounts of stress and anxiety that gets generated by startups and the startup world."[4]

Chris Tsai has experienced the weight of "huge amounts of stress and anxiety" firsthand. In 2012, Tsai and his team at Celery were accepted into Y Combinator, "the world's most powerful startup incubator."[5] Each year, Y Combinator (or YC for short) accepts two "batches" of startups, moves them out to Silicon Valley, and puts them through an intense three-month program where the founders are expected to work harder than they ever have before to build and refine their products. The program culminates in "Demo Day," where the startups pitch their businesses to a room full of investors and media—a true do-or-die moment for many of these companies. In YC's ten-year history, it has invested in some of Silicon Valley's greatest success stories, including Dropbox, Airbnb, and Reddit. But for every major success, there are a hundred companies that have achieved more moderate success or failed entirely. Of course, we all hear the rags-to-riches tales of YC's star startups, but we rarely hear about those that failed. "There are very few spectacular flameouts. The most common mode of failure is a company shrinking into a corner and dying," Tsai said to me.

A Christian who is following God's call to create, Tsai had a unique perspective to observe how his fellow YC "batchmates" responded to stress, adversity, and ultimately failure. Tsai shares, "In our batch of companies at YC, we just didn't know about the companies that failed. Founders just sort of hid it away. One day, you would ask yourself, 'I wonder what's going on with so and so company,' and then six months later you find out that the founders are all working on something new. That's when you realized they've failed or pivoted to another business idea. If your company fails, you don't want to talk about it. The nature of failure in Silicon Valley in some ways is covering it up, as opposed to Christians who may be more willing to be vulnerable."

Tsai's last comment got me thinking: Are Christians more vulnerable and transparent about our struggles and failures than the rest of the world? I don't think so. What's perhaps most ironic about Startup Funeral is that it was designed to mimic a church service, with a "pastor," bagpipes, and the congregants singing "Amazing Grace." But the fact is we in the actual church rarely respond to failure as if we understand that "Through many dangers, toils and snares, I have already come. 'Tis grace has brought me safe thus far, and grace will lead me home."[6]

This is a problem throughout the church, not just among those of us who are called to create. We come to church on Sunday mornings, put on a happy face, and pray that we never have to progress past small talk. "Hey, how are you? I loved the picture you posted on Instagram last night! Did you see the game yesterday?" Instead of treating our fellow church members as brothers and sisters in Christ, we have conversations that are not much deeper than those we carry on with the barista at our favorite coffee shop. Meanwhile, our marriages are failing at alarming rates, we are addicted to the adoration of people we don't care about on social media, and we carry the weight of a variety of hidden sins. For many of us, church has become a country club to showcase our best selves rather than a community that gathers to honestly share our struggles and failures, secure in the grace of our brothers and sisters and, ultimately, God.

Why aren't Christians more vulnerable? Why aren't those of us who are called to create open and honest about our struggles? Why do we try so desperately to ensure nobody sees our failures? Because at the end of the day, we aren't fully tapping into the gospel of Jesus Christ for our day-to-day functional salvation. Sure, we understand that it is "by grace [we] have been saved, through faith" (Eph. 2:8), relying on Christ's work on the cross for our ticket to heaven. But we live as though we still have something to prove, someone to impress, or something we need to do to demonstrate our worth. We treat the gospel as a "fire suit," great for keeping us out of hell but not much else. In reality, the gospel is the only thing that will allow us to face struggles and failures with true peace. In the words of pastor Timothy Keller, "Christians should be known to be calm and poised in the face of difficulty or failure. This may be the most telling way to judge if a person is drawing on the resources of the gospel in the development of personal character."[7]

> Because of the gospel, Christians can respond to adversity and failure with uncommon hope, transparency, and boldness.

For those of us who are called to create, some level of failure is inevitable. The nature of creating new things is that it is risky. In the words of pastor Erwin Mc-Manus, author of *The Artisan Soul*, "We cannot live to create and be surprised that we have traveled through failure."[8] Knowing that adversity and failures are coming our way, how are we, as Christians, to respond? Because of the gospel, we can respond with uncommon hope, transparency, and boldness.

Be Hopeful

In the 1860s, Chicago was booming, having quadrupled in population since 1850. The city's explosive growth attracted hordes of young, ambitious professionals to the Windy City, including a young Christian family of six whose patriarch was a prominent lawyer and a senior partner at one of Chicago's top law firms. In the spring of 1871, this man felt the call to create, and made substantial investments in the design and construction of new buildings throughout Chicago. But a few months later, his investments went up in flames as the Great Chicago Fire destroyed much of his real estate and the city. The loss was significant, but it paled in comparison to the tragedy the man would experience just two years later.

In 1873, the man and his wife decided to take their four daughters on an extended vacation to England, where their friend D. L. Moody was expected to be preaching in the fall. As the family was set to head to New York to board the ship to Europe, the man was forced to stay behind in Chicago to attend to a business matter. He encouraged his wife and daughters to go on without him, promising he would meet them in Europe as soon as possible. The five women made it safely to New York and boarded the *Ville du Havre*. As the ship was crossing the Atlantic, the women felt a sudden jolt. The *Ville du Havre* had been struck by an iron sailing vessel. Twelve minutes later, the ship sank to the bottom of the ocean, split in two. All four daughters died. Their mother was one of the few passengers to survive.

Upon arriving in England, she telegrammed her husband in Chicago. "Saved alone," she said. The husband left Chicago right away, sailing to England to meet his grieving wife. We don't know much about his journey across the Atlantic, but I have to imagine the man spent his days alone, grieving his loss and questioning his God. I can see him sitting, staring out the window at the infinite sea, reading the biblical account of Job, a man like him who had been blessed with so much—wealth, success, family—only to see it all taken away from him in the blink of an eye. We don't know much about what happened on that ship, but we do know this: as the ship crossed over the spot where the man's daughters were now resting in peace, Horatio Spafford took out his pen and wrote these words:

> When peace, like a river, attendeth my way,
> When sorrows like sea billows roll;
> Whatever my lot, Thou hast taught me to say,
> It is well, it is well with my soul.[9]

How could Spafford pen the line "It is well with my soul" without dousing the ink with his tears? He had hope. This hope wasn't rooted in himself, his ability to push through his suffering, or even the fact that his wife had miraculously survived the wreck and was waiting for him across the sea. No, as Spafford's classic hymn shows us, his hope was rooted in something far deeper. His hope was rooted in Jesus Christ and his work on the cross. As Spafford wrote in verses two and three:

> Though Satan should buffet, though trials should come,
> Let this blest assurance control,
> That Christ hath regarded my helpless estate,
> And hath shed His own blood for my soul.
>
> My sin, oh, the bliss of this glorious thought!
> My sin, not in part but the whole,
> Is nailed to His cross, and I bear it no more,
> Praise the Lord, praise the Lord, O my soul![10]

As he was sailing across the ocean mourning the loss of his children, Spafford was writing about the cross. Why? Because his hope was rooted in a God who understood his pain, a God who watched his own innocent Son die on a cross. Spafford clung to the fact that even the darkest event in history was used for his (and our) good, and for the glory of God. Without Jesus's death, all would not be well with Spafford's soul. But since God had demonstrated that even the gruesome death of his innocent Son could be used for his glory and our eternal good, Spafford and all of us have hope. Though trials should come, they, too, will be used for God's glory and our sanctification. In the words of Dietrich Bonhoeffer, "The fact that Jesus Christ died is more important than the fact that I will die. And the fact that Jesus Christ was raised from the dead is the sole ground of my hope."[11]

The trials you and I face personally and professionally will almost certainly pale in comparison to Spafford's. But our source of hope is the same. If you're late to ship your newest product, if you lose your biggest customer, if your art doesn't sell, even if your business completely fails, you can look to the cross as Spafford did and say, "It is well, it is well with my soul." Romans 8:28 reminds us that "We know that in all things God works for the good of those who love him, who have been called according to his purpose." For those who are called to create, failure and adversity are inevitable. But we, like Spafford, have hope that God is working everything for his glory and our good.

Be Transparent

I had done this enough times that I had come to expect the pre-speech nerves I was now feeling. But this was a whole new level. Before I took the stage at the Guardian's Activate Summit in New York City, I was able to calm my nerves long enough to appreciate the moment I was living. In a few minutes, I was to take the stage following an amazing "fireside chat" with Chris Hughes, a cofounder of Facebook and the leader of the Obama campaign's historic "My Barack Obama" social network. If that wasn't cool enough, the rest of the lineup of speakers at the event included the CEOs of the *New York Times*, the *Guardian*, and Tumblr; the CTO of Amazon.com; a general partner of Andreessen Horowitz; and a former United States senator. And then there was me, Jordan Raynor, a cofounder of a company no one could properly pronounce.

Fourteen months prior to this speech, my team and I launched Citizinvestor, a crowdfunding platform for local government projects. What followed was nothing short of a whirlwind of attention and adoration. In just over a year, our young company had been invited to the White House to talk about what implications crowdfunding might have on the federal government; we were featured alongside a movie starring Matt Damon; we had tea with the lieutenant governor of California; and we were featured in media such as *The Economist*, *Fast Company*, and CNBC. A week after my speech in New York, my wife and I would take a week-long, all-expenses-paid trip to France, where I had been invited to address the World Forum for Democracy about how Citizinvestor might work in Europe. I was living the entrepreneur's dream come true.

But when I slid across the backseat of the Uber car to head back to LaGuardia Airport after my speech, reality set back in. As my cofounder, Tony DeSisto, shut the cab door, we looked at each other, knowing what the other was thinking: *We need to sell the company.* While Citizinvestor had generated an unbelievable amount of attention and accolades, it was failing to generate the thing that matters most in a new venture: meaningful revenue. We knew we had enough financial capital to keep the company running for another year, and we had some ideas for new products that would generate significant revenue from the niche market we were beginning to win. But we also recognized that our brand wouldn't stay so hot forever, and there was a window of opportunity to try to land Citizinvestor within a larger acquiring company who could afford to invest the resources needed to make the product succeed. So there, in the back of our freezing-cold Uber, we strategized about how to fail on our own terms, through an acquisition of our young startup.

We spent the next twelve months seeking an acquirer for Citizinvestor, and while we came incredibly close a number of times, we never made a deal. Now, we were stuck. In the midst of seeking an acquiring company, we did launch a new product (Citizinvestor Connect) that was beginning to generate meaningful revenue, but it was too little too late. We were running out of money and we had to make a change if Citizinvestor was ever going to have a chance at survival. That's when I decided (or rather, was forced) to stop drawing a salary from the company and figure out my next move. As mentioned previously, through a lot of prayer and soul searching, God made it clear to me that my next move was to launch Vocreo, where I could help other entrepreneurs fulfill their call to create. As I sat down to write a blog post announcing my new venture, I knew I had to address the elephant in the room: Why was I leaving Citizinvestor, the company I had loved so publicly for the last three years? I knew that my departure was going to raise a lot of questions about the health of the company and my abilities as an entrepreneur, but instead of confronting those inquiries head-on, I adopted the old marketing maxim to "Tell the truth, nothing but the truth," but certainly not the whole truth. Here's how I couched my transition:

> Vocreo marks the third venture I have launched in my career, following the success of Direct Media Strategies in 2011, and most recently, Citizinvestor, which I have been focused on for almost three years. When Tony DeSisto first approached me with the idea of a "Kickstarter for government," I was skeptical, but I was curious enough to give the idea a shot. I'm so glad I did. Today, Citizinvestor is the largest crowdfunding platform for government projects in the United States with more than 185 government partners. And since the launch of Citizinvestor Connect in August 2014, the company's revenue has grown an astounding ten thousand percent and the business has found a self-sustaining model. This couldn't have been said six months ago.

What a load of crap. Yes, it was true that Citizinvestor was (and continues to be) the largest crowdfunding platform for government projects in the United States, but the whole truth is that all of our competition left the market because they weren't able to find a sensible business model. Yes, it was true that our revenue grew by more than ten thousand percent, but the whole truth is that when your revenue is essentially nothing, there's nowhere to go but exponentially up.

My point here is not that we who are called to create should voluntarily expose every ugly detail of every single failure. So, what *is* my point? The above paragraph was my rehearsal for a conversation I knew I was going to have dozens of times with friends, family, and colleagues in the months following my departure from Citizinvestor. Because my identity had become so wrapped up in my company and its success, I could not handle being transparent about the real reasons I was stepping away. Why does that matter? Because every time I regurgitated the above speech, I missed an opportunity to share the hope I have in Christ. What if, instead of selecting only the facts I wanted people to hear to make me look good, I had been transparent? I could have said, "Citizinvestor has had a great run. We are the only company left standing in a civic crowdfunding market we still believe in, and we have a great new product that is beginning to generate meaningful revenue. But unfortunately, we are running out of financial capital, and I can no longer afford to focus on the company full-time. Obviously, this is not what I wanted, but I am confident that God is using this for my good."

> Our response to failure and adversity can be one of the greatest opportunities for Christians to be set apart from the world.

Maybe someone would have asked the follow-up question, "How can you believe that God is using this for your good?" Maybe not. But I wish I had given people an opportunity to ask. I wish I had placed my identity in who God says I am rather than what other people think of me and my accomplishments. I wish I had given those around me a chance to see what Christ-rooted, Spafford-like hope looks like in the midst of professional failure. I wish I had believed God's promise that he will work everything for my good—which, by the way, he clearly has. Today, Citizinvestor is truly stronger than ever. By God's grace, the company has been able to generate enough revenue to stay in the black and, most recently, bring in a new CEO with decades of experience leading tech startups to IPOs and major acquisitions. But the greatest good that has come out of this failure for me is that God has had an opportunity to chisel away at the idols in my heart, making more room for him. As the authors of *Life Creative* reminded me, "Your sanctification is God's utmost desire for the whole of your life. Every bit of it!"[12] Even professional failure. I am convinced that our response to failure and adversity can be one of the greatest opportunities for Christian entrepreneurs and creatives to be set apart from the world, if only we are willing to be transparent.

Be Bold

Sajan George began his career turning around failing companies. But it didn't take long to spark an interest in George to apply his experience to fixing some of America's worst-performing schools. A managing director at a renowned consulting firm, George led the firm's education division, helping to turn around some of the nation's largest, urban K-12 public school districts, including ones in New York City, Washington, DC, and New Orleans.

But after a decade in this role, George was getting frustrated. He wanted to do more to fix the country's failing education system. That's when God used a film to grab hold of George's heart and call him to create. As he watched the premiere of *Waiting for Superman*, a documentary about America's declining public school system, tears filled George's eyes. "Those weren't my kids on the screen, but I felt a deep, deep sense of sadness," he said. "And I felt connected to what God must feel for those children when they're denied a decent educational opportunity. When I got home, I thought, 'I've got to go to the depth and bottom of this feeling. I've got to chase wherever it goes because there's something in that feeling that's the heart of God.'"[13]

George was beginning to sense God's call to create. He had the skills to be a successful entrepreneur, he was clearly passionate about solving America's education problem, and he was beginning to catch a vision for a new venture whereby he could reveal God's character and love others. George's search for what God was doing in his heart and America's education system led him to quit his high-paying job and launch Matchbook Learning, a nonprofit that helps turn around underperforming schools by giving teachers the technology they need to customize the educational experience for each and every student.

But three weeks after receiving his final paycheck from his previous employer, fear of failure started to settle in. As George remembered:

It was February 2011. I woke up and the house was quiet. . . . I'm lying in bed, and I realize I don't have anything to do that day . . . I literally have a completely blank calendar. And then this panic comes over me. . . . I'm having this conversation with myself, saying, "You are the stupidest man on the planet. We are deep in what is arguably our country's worst recession in decades, maybe ever. And you left a good-paying job. You have a wife and three kids to feed, and you have no plan." As the panic is setting in, two questions come to mind: "God, do you love me?" and "God, is it okay if I fail?" While I didn't hear an audible voice, I had a deep sense that the answer to both questions was "Yes." Once I had that sense, I got up out of bed, and I was good. I never looked back. I was okay. If the worst thing that happens is that I horribly, terribly, miserably fail, that's okay.[14]

George's experience reminds me of a scene from my all-time favorite TV show, *The West Wing*.[15] It's the day of the final debate of President Josiah Bartlet's political career, and the consensus is that if he wins the debate, Bartlet will win reelection to the presidency. The stakes couldn't be higher. Just before leaving the White House to head to the debate site, the president is asked to step outside the Oval Office for a quick word with his chief of staff, best friend, and quasi–father figure, Leo McGarry. In his final words to the president before he heads off to fight for four more years of power, McGarry says, "There's nothing you can do that's not going to make me proud of you. Eat 'em up. Game on." The president goes on to exceed sky-high expectations, crush his opponent in the debate, and win reelection.[16]

Just as Jesus needed to hear his Father say, "This is my beloved Son, in whom I am well-pleased," before he boldly launched his public ministry, we need to hear God speaking these words to us if we are to boldly build the ventures God has called us to create. We need to be reminded of our Father's "never stopping, never giving up, unbreaking, always and forever love" for us.[17] This should make us the boldest entrepreneurs on the planet! We truly have nothing to lose, for even if our ventures cause us to lose our lives, our death would be gain as we would be with Christ forever. Without this hope, failure is terrifying. But with it, you can genuinely say that whatever your lot—epic success, massive failure, or something in between—it is well with your soul.

9

renewing our minds

Stretching out his hands, Morpheus holds a blue pill in one palm and a red pill in the other, presenting Neo with a choice. "This is your last chance," Morpheus says. "After this, there is no turning back. You take the blue pill—the story ends, you wake up in your bed and believe whatever you want to believe. You take the red pill—you stay in Wonderland, and I show you how deep the rabbit hole goes."[1]

This scene from the 1999 blockbuster hit *The Matrix* is one that has been reimagined time and time again in film, television, and literature: Jack and Kate choose to leave the real world and go back to the island in *LOST*; Lucy decides to walk through the wardrobe in *The Lion, the Witch and the Wardrobe*; Jake chooses to live with the Na'vi on Pandora in *Avatar*. These are stories about choice—and more specifically, choosing between two worlds. In the case of *The Matrix*, Morpheus is asking Neo to choose between the real world and "the matrix," a world that appears to be reality but, in fact, is just a simulation.

Each of us who have been called to create are faced with a choice not that dissimilar to Neo's: we can choose to create for ourselves and live only for the life right in front of our eyes, or we can choose to reimagine our work as service to the One who has called us to create and "fix our eyes not on what is seen, but on what is unseen" (2 Cor. 4:18). But unlike the fictional choices of Neo and others, choosing to create for the glory of God does not magically remove us from our current world. There is no blue or red pill to transport us to an alternate reality. Regardless of the choice we make, we will remain in our current context and continue to do our work. It's the difference between virtual reality and augmented reality. No clue what I'm talking about? Stay with me for a minute.

The point of virtual reality—now being brought mainstream by Sony's Morpheus and Facebook's Oculus Rift headsets—is to convince users that they are in an entirely different world. When you strap on a virtual reality headset, a pair of goggles fits tightly over your eyes and headphones block out any audio from the real world. As the video and audio begin to play, you begin to feel as if you are immersed in another world. If you've ever watched someone experience virtual reality, you know what I'm talking about. Jaw dropped, the user is mesmerized and soon forgets you are there. Like the matrix, they are fully immersed in an alternate reality. Virtual reality's close but fundamentally different cousin is augmented reality, perhaps most famously demonstrated by Google Glass. *The Economist* explains the difference between the two:

If virtual reality is *The Matrix*, then augmented reality is *The Terminator*. Augmented reality . . . does not dispense with the real world, but uses computers to improve it in various ways. In *The Terminator*, Arnold Schwarzenegger's killer robot sees a constant stream of useful information laid over his view of the world, a bit like the heads-up displays used by fighter pilots.[2]

Instead of transporting a user to an entirely other world, augmented reality "maintains its users' connection with the real world,"[3] overlaying information on top of reality to change the user's perspective. This is the picture for us who choose to create for the One who has called us rather than for ourselves.

Make no mistake: you and I have a choice as to whom we will create for, and it's a choice that impacts so much of our entrepreneurial and creative endeavors. As we've seen, if we choose to reimagine our work as service to our Creator, it will change our motivations for creating, the products we create, and how we create them. It will lead us to prioritize people over profit and set the highest standard for excellence in everything we do. It will equip us to rest and respond honestly to adversity and failure. And, as we will see in the following chapters, it will reshape how we think about profit and what it means to make disciples.

If you are still reading this book, you have likely already made the decision to create not for yourself but for the One who has called you to create. That's great! But here's the challenge: everything around us tells us that the point of entrepreneurship, creativity, and life itself is to make a name for ourselves, to accumulate wealth, to build our personal brands, to cut costs at the expense of quality, and to view people as soulless transactions. If we choose to expend our creative energies sacrificially, we are choosing to be misunderstood and perhaps even mocked. In the words of the apostle Peter, we will be living as "aliens and strangers" in a world waiting to be redeemed and remade by the First Entrepreneur.

> If we are to thrive as entrepreneurs who create for the glory of God rather than ourselves, we will need to augment reality.

If we are to thrive as entrepreneurs who create for the glory of God rather than ourselves, we will need to augment reality. We will have to daily put on metaphorical lenses that overlay eternal truths over our world. How do we do that? Through the constant renewing of our minds. In Romans 12, immediately after Paul urges us to lay down our lives as a "living and holy sacrifice" to the One who has called us to create, he says, "And do not be conformed to this world, but be transformed by the renewing of your mind, so that you may prove what the will of God is, that which is good and acceptable and perfect" (Rom. 12:1–2 NASB).

How, practically, do we renew our minds and remind ourselves of our commitment to create to glorify our Creator and not ourselves? I would submit that we do this primarily through regular communion with God, our partners (both in marriage and in business), and other Christians, especially those who share our call to create.

Communing with God

Jonathan Cordeau slumped into the cramped seat on his flight to New York City, utterly exhausted. He had spent the last few months flying around the country, trying to raise capital for his online payments software startup, AcceptOn. But fundraising was not going well. Cordeau had his share of success in the past: his previous company had been accepted into 500 Startups (one of Silicon Valley's premier startup accelerators) and was eventually acquired. But lightning did not seem to be striking twice.

He pulled a *Fortune* magazine out of the seat pocket in front of him to find the CEO of one of his competitors on the cover. Shoving the magazine back, Cordeau pulled open his laptop to discover that Square, the payments giant founded by Twitter cofounder Jack Dorsey, had announced its plans to go public. To add insult to injury, when Cordeau touched down at LaGuardia, he was heading to meetings just blocks away from the New York Stock Exchange, where payments-processing leader First Data was celebrating their mammoth IPO. Everywhere Cordeau looked, his colleagues and competitors were attaining the very success that seemed so elusive to him.

"Sitting on that plane, I was beat down," Cordeau said. Frustrated, tired, and somewhat lost, he put his laptop away and did what he had done so many times before on his entrepreneurial journey: he pulled out his Bible. "I opened my Bible and randomly turned to Psalm 73, which I had never read before," Cordeau said, "but the Lord knew that these were the words I needed to hear. In verses 3–5 David says, 'For I envied the arrogant when I saw the prosperity of the wicked. They have no struggles; their bodies are healthy and strong. They are free from common human burdens; they are not plagued by human ills.' To paraphrase, the psalmist is basically crying out, 'Lord, why is everybody else so successful?'

I think this is something every entrepreneur struggles with at some point. I'm sitting on my flight thinking that everywhere I look, I see others succeeding. Why not me?"

As Cordeau continued reading, he found a model in David for how to maintain perspective and renew our minds through trying times:

> When I tried to understand all this,
> it troubled me deeply
> till I entered the sanctuary of God . . . .
> Yet I am always with you;
> you hold me by my right hand.
> You guide me with your counsel,
> and afterward you will take me into glory.
> Whom have I in heaven but you?
> And earth has nothing I desire besides you.
> My flesh and my heart may fail,
> but God is the strength of my heart
> and my portion forever.
> Those who are far from you will perish;
> you destroy all who are unfaithful to you.
> But as for me, it is good to be near God. (vv. 16, 23–28)

"As I finished that psalm, I was washed with thankfulness that the Lord showed me the eternal perspective I needed. That his promise is for my future, for eternity," Cordeau said. "I'd become caught up with the idea of worldly success, losing perspective of the opportunities he created for me, and his measure of success. His call is for us to walk humbly with him (Mic. 6:8), and to abide in him. It's impossible to maintain this eternal perspective without constant communion with the One who has called me to create."

How are the psalmist, Cordeau, and the rest of us able to maintain perspective and renew our minds as we create? Through intimate and regular communion with God. Of course, Jesus modeled this better than anyone in history. Talk about an "alien and stranger," Jesus was God himself, come to earth to dwell among us. Jesus knew better than anyone else the importance of communion with his Father for the sake of renewing his mind. The night before his crucifixion, Jesus could sense the horror of what was awaiting him at the cross. As he told his disciples, "My soul is deeply grieved, to the point of death" (Matt. 26:38 NASB). Jesus came to earth to serve, not to be served. He had made a choice to reimagine his work as a means of glorifying his Father, not himself. But even though that commitment had been made, Jesus the God-man needed constant communion with his Father to renew and refocus his mind. That night, Jesus went off alone into the Garden of Gethsemane three times to commune with his Father through prayer. Matthew records the scene:

> Going a little farther, he fell with his face to the ground and prayed, "My Father, if it is possible, may this cup be taken from me. Yet not as I will, but as you will." Then he returned to his disciples and found them sleeping. "Couldn't you men keep watch with me for one hour?" He asked Peter. "Watch and pray so that you will not fall into temptation. The spirit is willing, but the flesh is weak." He went away a second time and prayed, "My Father, if it is not possible for this cup to be taken away unless I drink it, may your will be done." When he came back, he again found them sleeping, because their eyes were heavy. So he left them and went away once more and prayed the third time, saying the same thing. (vv. 39–44)

If Jesus needed constant communion with God to renew his mind, how much more do we need to be spending regular time studying his Word and speaking to him through prayer? One of my favorite verses is 2 Corinthians 4:18, which says, "So we fix our eyes not on what is seen, but on what is unseen, since what is seen is temporary, but what is unseen is eternal." The word "fix" is active. It is something we must continually do. In order to avoid conforming to this world's way of thinking, we, like Cordeau and Jesus, must continually fix our minds on the One who has called us to create through regular study of his Word and prayer.

> If Jesus needed constant communion with God to renew his mind, how much more do we?

Communing with Partners

Just as Jesus took time to regularly commune with his Father, he also took time to commune with other believers, primarily his twelve disciples. But even within that relatively small group, Jesus had an even smaller group comprised of Peter, James, and John, with whom he communed more regularly and intimately (these were the disciples Jesus brought along to the Garden of Gethsemane in Matthew 26). This was Jesus's inner circle, his closest "partners" in his ministry. While communion with God and the larger body of believers is essential for renewing our mind, we would do well to follow Jesus's model of regularly communing with a small group of partners who know us intimately and can really challenge us to fix our eyes on the things of God as we create.

Tim Taylor has the unique perspective of having operated similar businesses with and without a partner. For nearly seven years, Taylor ran a video production studio on his own. The company did well and Taylor felt he was genuinely serving God and others through his work. As he entered his seventh year of business as a sole proprietor, Taylor's wife, Kristin Joy (the woman from chapter 1 who drove sixteen hours to thank the pastor who affirmed her creativity as being "central and of infinite worth"), approached him with an idea to combine his talents as a videographer with her considerable skills as a photographer to offer families and businesses a truly unique product that would artfully marry the two mediums. Tim agreed and jumped at the chance to work with his wife in their new venture, Pinwheel Pictures. Now the Taylors were not just partners in life, they were business partners too.

Sitting down at the Taylors' kitchen table, I asked Tim whether or not he could tell a difference in his ability to maintain eternal perspective since Kristin Joy joined him as his business partner. "The difference has been immense," Tim said. "Candidly, when I was running my business on my own, there were shortcuts I took that were morally shady. The easiest example to recall is pirating software. When Kristin Joy and I started Pinwheel Pictures, I didn't think twice about continuing to use the same pirated video editing software I had used for the first seven years of my career. Every videographer does it. But Kristin Joy immediately called me out, reminding me that while pirating the software saved us money, it was stealing. It was sin. Plain and simple. When I was on my own, I didn't have a partner to identify and call me out on blind spots like that one. Clearly, stealing software

was wrong. But I had done it for so long, I had become blind
to that particular sin. Kristin Joy helps spot my blind spots in
a loving way, rooted in her love of the Lord and our mutual
desire to run a business that glorifies Him."

What Tim has discovered is that partners—be they spouses,
business partners, or, as in Tim's case, both simultaneously—
know us better than any other human being. This allows for
a deeper level of intimacy, accountability, and opportunity
to renew each other's minds with spiritual truths. While the
Taylors help renew each other's minds regarding seemingly
"small" things, like the software they use, they lean on each
other for bigger struggles as well. Like many creative service
companies, the Taylors have a few clients that make up a
significant chunk of their annual revenue. "There's a temptation to be codependent on those clients," Kristin Joy said.
"There's one of our corporate clients in particular who we
love working with but are frequently anxious about retain-
ing. We find ourselves nervously wondering, 'Are they happy?
Did they love the last video we produced for them? Is there a
chance they would drop us for another vendor?' In those moments in which we find ourselves being emotionally enslaved
to a particular client, Tim and I renew each other's minds,
reminding each other that, while we love our client, they are
just someone the Lord is funneling work through. It is the
Lord working through them. He is the One who worked to
secure the client for us in the first place. If we know we have
done our very best work for the client and we still lose them,
then that's the Lord's will. The Lord gives, and the Lord
takes away. That truth gives us rest and allows us to detach
from the need of being emotionally or spiritually dependent
on any one client. But both Tim and I can forget truths like

these. That's why we have each other as partners: to remind each other of the Lord's promises."

Tim added, "We have made a choice to see our business spiritually, to create not for ourselves but for God and others. Spending time with the Lord each morning is what begins to give me this perspective. His Word reminds me of eternal truths I need as I start my day. But it is regular communion with other believers—particularly my wife and business partner—that renews my mind, reminding me of those truths throughout the day."

Communing with Other Believers

J. R. R. Tolkien had a thing for trees. So when he woke up one morning to find that a beloved tree just outside his home had been inexplicably chopped down by a neighbor, he was quite disturbed. But Tolkien's grief went deeper than mourning the loss of a single tree. For him, the fate the tree experienced represented what he feared for his "internal tree," The Lord of the Rings series. By this time, Tolkien had spent decades working on what he envisioned to be the crowning achievement of his career as an author. In painstaking detail, Tolkien spent years constructing imaginary languages and thousands of years of national histories that he felt were necessary to create the depth and texture needed to captivate readers of his epic fantasy trilogy. Tolkien's progress on the project had slowed as World War II crescendoed across Europe, and although Tolkien was in his fifties, with no chance of being drafted into military service, invasion of Britain seemed imminent and Tolkien began to despair that, like the tree, his life might be suddenly chopped down along with his life's work.

Fortunately for Tolkien, a devout follower of Christ, he had surrounded himself with a community of other Christians to help renew his mind and maintain his eternal perspective. This group of friends, known as "the Inklings," was composed of some of the world's greatest Christian minds, including Charles Williams, Hugo Dyson, Owen Barfield, and, most notably, C. S. Lewis and his brother, Warnie. Each of these men shared Tolkien's love of the Lord and literature; each of them followed God's call to create through their writings. From the early 1930s until late 1949, the group met with varying regularity. Most Tuesdays, you could find them informally gathered in the back corner of an Oxford pub called The Eagle and Child, which you can still visit today. There was no formal agenda for these meetings, for this was primarily a gathering of good friends, what we Western Christians today might call a "small group." Speaking of the influence the group had on his life, C. S. Lewis, who was led to faith in Christ by Tolkien and Dyson, said, "What I owe to them all is incalculable. Is there any pleasure on earth as great as a circle of Christian friends by a good fire?"[4]

At their regular get-togethers, the Inklings would read their latest writings, get feedback (often harsh), drink a pint of beer, and help renew each other's minds with regards to their Christian faith. At one of these meetings, we know that Tolkien brought up the tree that had been chopped down outside his home and the fear he had that The Lord of the Rings series might suffer the same fate.[5] Like many times before, the Inklings' subsequent conversation undoubtedly helped renew Tolkien's mind concerning what it means to succeed and fail in this life. With this biblically grounded perspective from his friends, Tolkien wrote a short story titled

"Leaf by Niggle," clearly an autobiographical metaphor for his "internal tree."

Niggle was a painter who one day caught a vision for a painting of a leaf. Over time, his vision expanded to that of a whole tree, and then, beyond the tree, an entire country with forests and snow-capped mountains. Like Tolkien with The Lord of the Rings, Niggle's vision for this painting captured his imagination so much that he lost interest in all his other paintings. Sensing his mortality, Niggle committed to focusing intently on finishing his magnum opus before his death.

Niggle worked diligently but he never accomplished much, for he was a perfectionist, spending days and weeks on a single leaf, "trying to catch its shape, and its sheen, and the glistening of dewdrops on its edges."[6] One night, Niggle came down with a fever, and knowing the end of his life was near, he worked frantically to finish his masterpiece. But it was too little, too late. As death closed in, Niggle burst into tears, realizing his life's work would go unfinished.

After his death, some of Niggle's neighbors were looking through his house when they stumbled upon the crumbling canvas Niggle had erected for his masterpiece. Only "one beautiful leaf" remained intact. The neighbors had the leaf framed and placed in the town museum, "and for a long while 'Leaf: by Niggle' hung there in a recess, and was noticed by a few eyes. But eventually the Museum was burnt down, and the leaf, and Niggle, were entirely forgotten in his old country."[7]

Without the Inklings' influence on Tolkien's life, the story may have ended there. But because Tolkien had surrounded himself with a community of fellow believers, he was able to continually renew his mind and refresh his perspective on the world, his work, and that of Niggle.

As Tolkien tells it, after Niggle's death, he was put on a train bound for the mountains of the heavenly afterlife. As he approached the outskirts of the heavenly country, something caught Niggle's eye. He hopped off the train and ran toward it.

> Before him stood the Tree, his Tree, finished. If you could say that of a Tree that was alive, its leaves opening, its branches growing and bending in the wind that Niggle had so often felt or guessed, and had so often failed to catch. He gazed at the Tree, and slowly he lifted his arms and opened them wide. . . . All the leaves he had ever laboured at were there, as he had imagined them rather than as he had made them; and there were others that had only budded in his mind, and many that might have budded, if only he had had time.[8]

Without constant communion with other believers to refresh their eternal perspectives, Tolkien may have never completed The Lord of the Rings, and Lewis may have never finished his Chronicles of Narnia. As we create in this world, it takes regular communion with our fellow brothers and sisters in Christ to renew our minds and refresh the lens through which we view the world. As pastor Timothy Keller, author of the magnificent *Every Good Endeavor*, points out:

> It takes regular communion with fellow believers to renew our minds and refresh the lens through which we view the world.

> Artists and entrepreneurs can identify very readily with Niggle. They work from visions, often very big ones, of a world they can uniquely imagine. Few realize even a significant percentage of their vision, and even fewer claim to have come close. If this life is all there is, then everything

will eventually burn up in the death of the sun and no one will even be around to remember anything that has ever happened. Everyone will be forgotten, nothing we do will make any difference, and all good endeavors, even the best, will come to naught. Unless there is God. If the God of the Bible exists, and there is a True Reality beneath and behind this one, and this life is not the only life, then every good endeavor, even the simplest ones, pursued in response to God's calling, can matter forever.[9]

Tolkien's story is one of community and how, through regular fellowship with other Christians, especially those who share our call to create, we can renew our minds and refresh the lenses by which we view the world. But the story *within* the story is one about perspective in the midst of challenges. Like Niggle, we all find our work challenging. Managing the tension between trusting and hustling is hard. Responding honestly to failure requires uncomfortable vulnerability the world is not used to seeing. And regularly communing with God and other believers takes commitment and the sacrifice of precious time. These are challenges unique to those of us who are called to create. But unlike Niggle, frantically despairing over his unfinished work, we know the end of the story. We have the "peace of God, which surpasses all comprehension" (Phil. 4:7 NASB) because we know that "there is a True Reality beneath and behind this one, and this life is not the only life."[10] That eternal perspective, constantly renewed through communion with God, our partners, and other believers, is essential as we move into the final part of this book to receive our charge.

PART 4

charge

10

commanded to create disciples

Contrary to the wishes of many Christians, God does not hand us clear answers to many of life's biggest questions: which career path to take, who to marry, which university to attend, and so forth. Much of the Christian life is a process of seeking God and discerning his will. But while God gives us the freedom to discern his calling in many areas of life, there are others that are not up for discussion where the Bible clearly commands us to act. One of these commands comes in Jesus's final words to his disciples before ascending to heaven: "Therefore go and make disciples of all nations, baptizing them in the name of the Father and of the Son and of the Holy Spirit, and teaching them to obey everything I have commanded you" (Matt. 28:19–20).

God has given us great freedom to discern where he has called us to work. Some will be called to law, some to medicine, some to finance. Some of us have been called to create! But regardless of where God has called you to expend your productive energies, all of us have been commanded to create disciples.

On my wedding day, five of my best friends stood next to me as I married Kara Goskie. Of those five friends, three of them now work full-time for churches or missions organizations: My brother-in-law Caleb is a super-talented sound and lighting technician at his church, my buddy Ryan is a disciple-making machine in his role as a student pastor in Jacksonville, Florida, and my friend Josh is an exceptional pilot who flies missionaries in and out of Papua New Guinea. For years, it was clear to me how these men were fulfilling the Great Commission. It was less clear how I was creating disciples in my work as an entrepreneur. My confusion was rooted in a misunderstanding of Jesus's command. For the longest time, I assumed that the operative word in the Great Commission was "Go," the implication being that in order to fulfill this command, I, like my friends, had to pack my bags and leave my professional, cultural, and geographic context in order to make disciples. This was part of the inner struggle I mentioned in chapter 3, when I was weighing the options of planting a church or starting another company. Deep down, I knew that Jesus couldn't possibly have meant that every single Christian was meant to travel to the most remote areas of the world to serve as a "full-time missionary." Dr. Kennon Vaughan, a pastor and the founder of discipleship training organization Downline Ministries, helped me understand Jesus's words:

> Regardless of where God has called you to work, all of us have been commanded to create disciples.

"Go" is not a command. [Jesus] is not commanding them to go, as much as he is saying, "Having gone . . . turn men into disciples!" The word "Go" literally means "having gone." The going is assumed. In other words, Jesus is going to adjourn the meeting on the hillside in Galilee, and he's saying, "Having gone from here, as you go, turn men into disciples." "Go" is not the command. If it were, then Jesus himself wasn't real big on fulfilling the Great Commission. Lest I be a heretic, hear me again: "Go" is not the command. Jesus didn't go more than two hundred miles away from his own hometown, and yet he is saying go make disciples of all nations, and I would venture to say Jesus is the greatest disciple maker in the history of the world. It wasn't about how far he went. It was about what he did while he was going. The same is true for you and I.[1]

The Great Commission is not necessarily calling you to move to the other side of the world to create disciples. It is, however, commanding you and me to create disciples as we go throughout life, from wherever God has called us today. For those who have been called to create, that means using our endeavors as a vehicle for creating disciples.

As entrepreneurs, we have a unique opportunity to join God in the work of creating followers of Christ. As we saw in chapter 2, God has called all of humankind to work. But who does he use to create those jobs? God has graciously given that awesome privilege to entrepreneurs! We are responsible for designing a world in which people will spend one-third of their waking hours. We are responsible for the values they see demonstrated throughout our organizations, the ideas they come in contact with, and the Christian character they see (or don't see) modeled. For many nonbelievers, the office is the only place they will regularly interact with Christians. Do we feel the weight of the awesome responsibility and opportunity set before us to allow God to use our ventures to turn men and women into disciples of Jesus Christ?

Perhaps no member of the early church took the responsibility of discipleship more seriously than the apostle Paul. His zeal for the gospel jumps off the pages of the New Testament. Given his passion for his work as a disciple-maker, it is worth examining why Paul often refused financial support that would allow him to preach full-time, choosing instead to continue to use his platform as an entrepreneur to create disciples.

The Apostle Paul

Paul understood something I think a lot of us get wrong today: that discipleship begins well before someone becomes a Christian. Too often today we see discipleship as only the process by which existing Christians become more like Christ: you "pray the prayer," fill out a card in the back of a pew, and someone from the church contacts you to "be discipled" by a more mature believer. This doesn't appear to be how Jesus thought about creating disciples. In his first exchange with the apostles, he said, "Follow me, and I will make you fishers of men." It would be another three years before we could say the apostles had a "conversion" experience, but Jesus was discipling them from the very beginning, intentionally investing in these men for the purpose of making them more like him. Paul, "called to be an apostle of Christ Jesus," understood Jesus's model for discipleship and used his tentmaking business to carry it out, first by loving people, then by speaking the gospel, and finally by teaching the Word.

After Paul's dramatic conversion experience on the road to Damascus, his contemporaries would have understood if he abandoned his trade as a tentmaker to spread the gospel as a full-time, donor-supported missionary. As 1 Corinthians 9 shows us, that was certainly an option for Paul, but he chose to create disciples as he was going about his work as an entrepreneur. Why? Mark Russell provides excellent insight into Paul's thinking here in *The Missional Entrepreneur*:

> Paul sought to build real-world relationships. He wanted to develop relationships with people because he knew that this is how the [gospel] is spread. He used all of the connections available in the vast network of business relationships to promote and spread the gospel. Paul said, "I have become all things to all men, so that by all possible means I might save some" (1 Cor. 9:22). This quote concludes his explanation and justification of why he did not work as a donor-supported minister. This shows that Paul did not do this because he had to or because he wanted to—rather this was Paul's strategy! According to the obvious flow of this passage, this is Paul's climactic reason for working rather than taking support. He worked in order to become all things to all people.[2]

Paul viewed his business as a vehicle to build relationships with and love people, both Christians and non-Christians alike. Paul knew that the gospel must be spoken to non-Christians and continually taught to believers, but he also knew that it must first be lived out through love of his fellow man. Just as Jesus broke bread with his disciples, worked alongside them, and spent time simply conversing with them, Paul understood that in order to properly communicate the gospel with words, he would first have to do it with actions, loving the people around him and modeling Christian character. Russell says, "What better way for people to see his character day in and day out than by working alongside them? This is surely one of the primary reasons why Paul chose to work in tent making."[3]

> To properly communicate the gospel with words, we must first do it with actions.

While Paul was intentional about first loving those he worked with, he also knew that it was necessary to speak the gospel in words. There's an old saying, often attributed to St. Francis, that says, "Preach the gospel always; if necessary use words." In the words of the authors of *The Gospel at Work*, "That sounds nice but it's nonsense. You have to use words if you want to preach the gospel. After all, it's good news. And sharing news requires words."[4] I couldn't have said it better myself, and I think Paul would agree. Dr. T. G. Soares writes that New Testament accounts of Paul's ministry "suggest the constant personal evangelism that Paul must have carried on during his hours of labor with the various fellow-workers with whom he was thrown into companionship."[5] Paul lived out the gospel, demonstrating the love of Christ to those he worked with. But he also undoubtedly used words to explain why he lived the way he did, speaking gospel truth to non-Christians he worked with, bringing them to saving faith in Christ.

Finally, Paul provides a model for what it looks like to use our work as entrepreneurs to continually teach the Word of God to fellow believers, discipling them to become more like Christ. Upon arriving in Corinth from Athens, Paul met a husband and wife team of fellow tentmakers named Aquila and Priscilla. Because of their common trade and belief in Jesus Christ, Paul stayed with the couple and worked alongside them. Again, Russell is worth quoting at some length:

> When Priscilla and Aquila met Paul they were probably already Christians. However, undoubtedly Paul took them deeper in the faith. It is very possible that Paul taught them how to blend workplace excellence and effective evangelism. They became tentmaking missionaries themselves, traveling on to Ephesus no doubt still practicing their trade and teaching the Way to people like Apollos. Paul modeled teaching in the context of daily life, which made spiritual instruction seem natural and flowing rather than forced and uncomfortable as it is commonly perceived. Due to this style, Paul created a positive feedback cycle that enabled exponential growth. His converts became teachers and their converts became teachers and the positive feedback cycle continued. While Paul clearly sought to turn converts into missionaries, he did not necessarily call them to pack up and go. Rather he encouraged them to live out their faith wherever they were. Paul did not have to continually exhort his students to be evangelists. He simply modeled and taught in such a way that evangelism seemed a normal and natural part of being a fully devoted follower of Christ. Too often being an evangelist is thought of as a specific and unique calling of God on an elected remnant of especially devout people. Paul's life and teaching exclaim the opposite: everyone should be a missionary in his daily life, just where he is.[6]

The apostle Paul provides a model for us to follow as we seek to create disciples through our own entrepreneurial endeavors, living out the gospel by loving people and building genuine relationships, speaking the gospel with words, and teaching the Word to fellow believers so that they might become more like Christ. But what does that look like today for those of us who are called to create? The following three entrepreneurs provide us with excellent examples.

Love People

As Dennis Hardiman's plane took off, he looked out the window at the foreign land below, thankful for the work God did through him and others on this missions trip. This was a fairly regular trip for Hardiman, who traveled multiple times a year to serve people in different cultures and share the name of Jesus. It's easy to see how this work is considered ministry; but as Hardiman will tell you, he sees no difference in this work and the work that waits for him back home at the mortgage company in which he serves as chairman of the board. To Hardiman, all of his work comes down to loving people by developing them personally, professionally, and spiritually and using that process to create disciples of Jesus Christ.[7]

Founded by Hardiman in 1983, Embrace Home Loans is one of the fastest-growing private companies in the United States. It is also one of America's favorite places to work, as evidenced by both *Entrepreneur* and *Fortune* magazine naming the company one of the "50 Best Small & Medium Companies to Work for in America" seven of the last eleven years. If you walk the halls of Embrace's headquarters, the overjoyed employees lead you to believe you're at a tech startup in Silicon Valley, not a mortgage company in Rhode Island. Why do people love working at Embrace so much? One of the company's core values gives a clue: "Invest in the professional and personal development of each other."

When Hardiman speaks about Embrace, he rarely talks about the company's size or impressive growth trajectory. A coach at heart, Hardiman is happiest when talking about how Embrace is getting better at loving its employees by helping them improve all areas of their lives. For Hardiman, this is not simply a means of making his employees more productive. His love of developing people stems from a rich understanding of God's desire to redeem human beings. "Business can be highly relevant to human development and our relationship with God," Hardiman said. "In business, you have an opportunity to help people navigate personal change—to realize their potential. For me, that's about redemption. As a Christian, I've found that the genius of how best to develop people is found in the truths of the Bible and in the person of Jesus."

Biblical truths are integrated deeply into how Embrace develops its people. As Hardiman and his team use these truths to help people realize their full potential, their employees are becoming more like they were created to be. They are becoming more like Christ. Hardiman and his team are doing the work of creating disciples even before speaking the name of Jesus, and they are doing it in a way that loves the whole person and does not just seek to convert someone and move on.

Hardiman's approach to discipleship follows that of Paul's: loving people first and then allowing the Lord to pave the way for speaking the gospel. As Hardiman said, "When you have conversations about people's development and you focus on the whole person, not just specific job functions, you build truly intimate relationships. At Embrace, we try to understand the limits our team members are facing that might stem from belief systems, thoughts that they hold, or attitudes they might have. When you start having conversations around these things, intimacy and vulnerability is the natural result. That gives freedom to connect at a much deeper level, person to person. The person of faith who is involved in those conversations and is supporting people in their development has an enormous opportunity to share matters of faith in the context of how it might be relevant to the specific personal challenges someone is facing. That's a much more effective model for creating disciples because it is genuinely loving and caring for people rather than pushing an agenda."

Hardiman doesn't walk the halls of Embrace with the sole plan of explicitly speaking the gospel to each and every employee. "I hold the agenda of seeking to be a blessing to my employees and to those around me," he said. For Hardiman, developing his employees is not just a means to an end of speaking the gospel. It is an end in and of itself because it is an act of love. As Hardiman and the apostle Paul show us, genuinely loving people often precedes an opportunity to speak the gospel.

That said, Hardiman recognizes the need to speak the gospel with words, not just actions. "In order to connect the dots between human development and helping someone know God, it obviously needs to be done in an explicit way. At some point, a conversation has to take place," he said. "But I think the best way to put someone on a path to seeking God is by showing them genuine love. We do that by helping develop the whole person. Through the process of developing our employees professionally, personally, and spiritually, people taste what is good. They taste truth. And over time, that changes the direction of their lives. It helps people realize they want something better. Oftentimes, that moves people into a form of seeking spiritual truth."

When we love the people who surround our ventures, be they employees, customers, or partners, we build intimacy and trust. In relationships like these, speaking the good news of Jesus Christ is simply a natural extension of our genuine care.

> Speaking the good news of Jesus Christ is simply a natural extension of our genuine care for others.

Speak the Gospel

Through a series of events, Ron and Dawn Marshall sensed God calling them to leave their home in the United States to go make disciples in Thailand. Eager to speak the gospel to the Thai people, the Marshalls learned the native language and got plugged into a local church in Chiang Mai. As they began exploring strategies for sharing the gospel in the predominantly Buddhist country, the Marshalls asked their fellow congregants how they could best serve the Thai people. Over and over again, they heard the same reply: find a way to provide jobs.

Ron was a former tire salesman and didn't consider himself to be an entrepreneur. At first, he didn't know how he would create jobs for the Thais. But that changed when the Lord clearly called Ron to create through a phone call from his former boss, who was looking to move some data-entry work offshore. Ron immediately saw an opportunity to provide jobs for the Thai Christians and a vehicle for speaking the gospel to non-Christians. As Ron said to his wife, "I can't believe I never thought of this before, but I think this business could be a real blessing to Thailand. We can give jobs to people who need it. They can then take care of their families and give money to the churches. This will help the church's financial situation and reduce the dependency on foreign donations. After we get going, maybe we can find a way to employ some non-Christians. It seems to me that it takes a long time for people to become Christians around here. The office could be a place for them to learn gradually over an extended period of time."[8]

Like Hardiman, the Marshalls believe that discipleship began with "blessing" others and living the gospel out through genuine love and care for people—providing them with jobs, dignity, and community. Ron took a genuine interest in the lives of his employees rather than walking in with an agenda to convert on day one. But while he took a "blessing first" mentality to his work as an entrepreneur, Ron never stopped looking for opportunities to clearly speak the gospel through words. Over time, the genuine community Ron built opened the door for employees to discuss spiritual things, and his Buddhist employees began asking questions about Christianity. Due to the flood of interest, Ron started a weekly Bible study at the office, knowing the Thais would feel much more comfortable studying the Bible there than in a church where they would risk being seen and shamed by their Buddhist relatives. Over the course of seven profitable years, the Marshalls' business provided jobs for forty-five people in Chiang Mai, twelve of whom are now followers of Jesus Christ!

How did the Marshalls produce such tremendous economic and spiritual fruit? That's the question Mark Russell sought to answer by closely studying the Marshalls and eleven other Christian-led enterprises in Chiang Mai:

> When asked the primary motivation for their work, the missionaries [like the Marshalls] who operated sustainable businesses that produced missional fruit tended to give comprehensive, holistic explanations for why they engaged in business as mission. They frequently used the term *bless*, which is why I describe their attitude as a blessing orientation. Their answers reflected a sincere concern for the Thai people, a desire to help people in many aspects of their lives, including financial (income), relational (family), and spiritual (understanding the Christian message and becoming Christ followers). In contrast, when asked their primary motivation, the missionaries who operated businesses that were struggling financially and producing little or no missional fruit gave conversion-oriented responses. They would use terms such as *convert* and *evangelism*. I frequently heard the phrase "We have to keep the main thing the main thing," meaning that the business and its corresponding social contribution to the lives of Thai people was only of instrumental value. The purpose of the business was to create an avenue for the missionaries to proclaim the Christian message and produce conversions. Ironically, these missionaries reported far fewer incidences of evangelism than those with a blessing orientation. Comparing six blessing companies versus six converting companies, the ratio difference was 48 to 1 in terms of conversions. The converting companies counted 1 conversion after the expenditure of 32 missionary years. In the blessing companies there were 36 conversions after the expenditure of 24 missionary years.[9]

The lesson here is one of sequence: in order to produce the most fruit in creating disciples through our ventures, we must first love people, taking a genuine interest in their lives and focusing on "blessing" rather than just "converting." Only then will we build the trust necessary to speak the gospel to those eager to hear it.

Through their business, the Marshalls employed a missions strategy known as "business as mission" (BAM), which has seen a rise in popularity in recent years. In general, BAM refers to for-profit ventures intentionally leveraged for creating disciples of Jesus Christ. Oftentimes, missionaries like the Marshalls will use BAM as a tool for sharing the gospel in countries traditionally hostile to Christianity. But, as I hope you see by now, it's not just people who move to a foreign land like the Marshalls who are on business as mission. Everyone who is called to create is on a mission to reveal God's character, love others, and, yes, create disciples. To do this well, we would be wise to follow the Marshalls' model, first loving people and then speaking the gospel clearly. Finally, if the Lord wills, we will have an opportunity to use our ventures to continually teach the Word of God to those around us, helping them become more like Christ.

Teach the Word

As the glass door to the conference room swung open, I was giddy. Somehow, my team and I had secured a meeting to pitch our product to my dream client: Chick-fil-A. As my colleague and I took our seats, eager to jump into the zooming Prezi pitch deck we had prepared, the head of Chick-fil-A's digital marketing team asked, "So, what's your story?" The question caught us off-guard. For starters, my colleague and I weren't sure which of us he had directed the question to. But more than that, this was not a question we were accustomed to hearing before we pitched our product. After exchanging awkward glances for what felt like two minutes, I took the bait, fumbling through some incoherent answer about my somewhat sad, lifelong obsession with Chick-fil-A. After the meeting, I reflected on the odd question, and the more I thought about it, the more I loved it. Our contact at Chick-fil-A did not see us as just another potential vendor. He saw us as people—people with a story worth listening to.

I now know that this question is a standard one within Chick-fil-A culture. A few years ago, Chick-fil-A produced a video titled "Every Life Has a Story," which is shown to new employees during training.[10] The video takes the viewer on a slow-motion tour through a Chick-fil-A restaurant, stopping to focus in on the faces of the store's customers and employees as text pops up to tell their stories. A teenage team member smiles at guests from behind the counter as we learn that she has just been "accepted into the college of her dreams." A "single mom raising a family alone and trying to make ends meet" takes a break as her two boys dig into their Chick-fil-A kids' meals. An elderly woman sits alone drinking a cup of coffee as we learn that her "husband of forty-nine years died last month. Today would've been their fiftieth anniversary." As the video fades to black, Chick-fil-A's newest employees are reminded that "Every life has a story . . . if we bother to read it."[11]

Chick-fil-A has been teaching their employees how to read the stories of the people around them for decades. The company's franchisees (known as operators) take seriously the job of teaching their largely teenage staff how to care for and love others. Whether these kids know it or not, they are being taught to become more like Christ. The operators who do this intentionally are using their businesses to create disciples, following the example set by Chick-fil-A's founder, Truett Cathy.

It's well known that all Chick-fil-A restaurants are closed on Sundays. And while this is partially to allow the company's employees to worship if they so choose, the origins of this policy stem from something much more practical. When Cathy was starting up the chain of quick-service chicken restaurants in the 1940s, he was already committed to teaching Sunday school to teenage boys at his church. While Cathy worked incredibly hard starting up Chick-fil-A, discipling these young men was important to him—so important that he chose to sacrifice a full day of profits each week to spend time with them. But it wasn't just at church that Cathy taught God's Word to these boys. He also used his restaurants as a means of discipling them, using Chick-fil-A's delicious food to incentivize the young men to attend regular Bible studies at the store.

Cathy understood what hundreds of Chick-fil-A operators have come to learn over the decades: that business can be a powerful means of teaching people (especially young people, in Chick-fil-A's case) biblical truths. As Cathy wrote in his autobiography:

> The restaurant business gives us a wonderful opportunity to mentor young people and help guide them toward adulthood. Hundreds of thousands of teenagers have worked at a Chick-fil-A restaurant, and I like to think we have been a positive influence for each of them. Chick-fil-A Operators take special care in selecting and working with teenagers who work in their restaurants, modeling for them positive character traits.[12]

One of those operators is Alex Clark, a faithful disciple of Cathy but more importantly of Jesus Christ. Just as I was asked "What's your story?" while being interviewed as a prospective Chick-fil-A vendor, Clark asks the same question of everyone he interviews for a job at his restaurant. Usually, Clark hears answers about where interviewees grew up, where they go to school, or what they hope to do in the future. But when he interviewed Jenny[13] for an entry-level team member position, she demurred, breaking eye contact and offering only the vaguest details of her life. Clark knew there was something she wasn't telling him, but he decided to give her a shot anyway.

Shortly after she picked up her uniform and started taking orders as a cashier, Clark received a call notifying him that Jenny was a felon on probation. "There's more to Jenny than you think," the caller said. Soon after that phone call, Jenny shared the rest of her story with Clark. Jenny had worked as a prostitute, been imprisoned for drug distribution, been divorced, and was now caring for her young child. Before coming to work for Clark, she had transitioned out of a rehabilitation facility, and now she was looking for a fresh start. Clark was reading the story of Jenny's life, but instead of shutting the book, he turned the page, hoping that Chick-fil-A could be the home Jenny needed for restoration.

As he did with all of his employees, Clark worked to develop Jenny professionally, personally, and spiritually. Eventually, Jenny worked her way up to a manager position in Clark's restaurant, joining the leadership team for that Chick-fil-A. For Clark, this is where serious discipleship happens. "My priority in my store is building genuine community among my leadership team," he said. "During our weekly leadership team meetings, I ask each member of the team to share something personal. I usually try to get the conversation started by posing a question such as, 'What's one thing about your life that you want to change?' Their answers are rarely about compensation or professional advancement. They go much deeper than that, discussing issues with their families or their purpose in life. During these meetings, I also give them an opportunity to ask me any question they want. On more than one occasion, a member of my team has asked me, 'Why do you do what you do?' or 'What is your purpose in life?' I love this question, as it allows me to easily share my faith and my motivation for creating new value through Chick-fil-A. I tell my team, 'My purpose in life is to enjoy and display my relationship with Christ for the joy of all people. Like Christ, I want to be a life-giving person. I want people to enjoy being around me so that they can catch a glimpse of what God is doing in my life.'"

During her time working for Clark, Jenny certainly caught a glimpse of what God was doing in Clark's life, as well as her own. As Clark shares, "During her time in my restaurant, Jenny was learning how to be a better professional, but she was also learning about love. She was learning that there are people who really loved her and cared for her. She was learning about grace, and she was experiencing genuine community." While working for Clark, Jenny started attending church regularly and studying God's Word. Then, one day, to Clark's delight, she came to him and shared that just as he had discipled her—loving her, speaking biblical truths to her, and teaching her God's Word—she wanted to begin discipling others.

Jenny was soon back in a courtroom, but instead of facing judgment, she stood before a group of juvenile delinquents sharing her story of redemption and how Christ was now graciously standing in as her advocate. Today, Jenny has an even greater platform to disciple others as she was recently promoted to the position of general manager at another Chick-fil-A.

By loving people, speaking the gospel, and teaching God's Word, we can experience the joy of seeing those around us become more like Christ.

"Jenny is a totally different person than when I hired her," Clark shared. "Did I have a part in that? I think God was working through us at Chick-fil-A, allowing us to teach the gospel through both our actions and our words."

Just as God worked through Hardiman's, the Marshalls', and Clark's entrepreneurial endeavors, he can work through yours and mine. It's time to stop thinking about discipleship as something we exclusively do on the weekends or when we are on a missions trip. "As we are going" about building our organizations, we are working alongside people Jesus has commanded us to turn into his disciples. By genuinely loving people, speaking the gospel, and continually teaching God's Word, we can experience the joy of seeing those around us become more like Christ.

11

the purpose of profit

When our entrepreneurial endeavors are successful, what are we to do with the profits? First, let me be clear about what I mean by the word *profit*. For the sake of this chapter, let's define profit as anything more than what your endeavor needs to sustain itself after making fair distributions to shareholders. If you are the sole shareholder in your business, we are talking about any financial gain above what you need to support yourself and your family. We are talking about abundance. I have no interest in nor the authority to suggest a particular income amount that is acceptable to meet your specific needs. That is between you and God. But I will state the obvious: the vast majority of Western Christians today (myself included) are living on far more income than we truly need to sustain our lives and our ventures. We live more abundantly than any human beings in the history of the world. So, what are we who are called to create to do with that abundance? The

answer to that question depends largely on our view of who
owns our ventures in the first place.

You Didn't Build That

On a hot July day in 2012, President Barack Obama took
the stage in Roanoke, Virginia, to campaign for reelection. It
was here that Obama made one of the most famous remarks
of the entire presidential contest, saying:

> If you've been successful, you didn't get there on your own.
> I'm always struck by people who think, well, it must be
> because I was just so smart. It must be because I worked
> harder than everybody else. If you were successful, some-
> body along the line gave you some help. There was a great
> teacher somewhere in your life. Somebody helped to create
> this unbelievable American system that we have that allowed
> you to thrive. Somebody invested in roads and bridges. If
> you've got a business—you didn't build that. Somebody else
> made that happen.[1]

As the words were coming out of the president's mouth,
the Romney campaign went into high gear, attacking the
president for suggesting that entrepreneurs are not the ones
who produce wealth. In response to the president's comments, Mitt Romney said, "To say that Steve Jobs didn't
build Apple, that Henry Ford didn't build Ford Motors, that
Papa John didn't build Papa John's Pizza . . . to say something like that, it's not just foolishness. It's insulting to every
entrepreneur, every innovator in America."[2]

Romney was right about one thing: almost nothing is more
insulting to the American idol of self than the insinuation

that entrepreneurs aren't solely responsible for their success. Romney's response fired up his base, and the Republican Party turned the line into a central theme of the fall campaign. As I sat in the crowd at the 2012 Republican National Convention, waiting for Romney to take the stage to accept his party's nomination for president amid an avalanche of red, white, and blue balloons, I was taken aback by how prominent this idea had become in the month since President Obama made those comments. Almost every speaker at the convention referenced the "gaffe," and the phrase "We Built It" was plastered prominently on the navy wall behind me for all the TV cameras to see.

Can I let you in on a little secret? Political affiliations aside, I cringed every time I heard Republicans attack the president for saying, "You didn't build that." Why? Because we *didn't* build that. As we saw in chapter 7, we are not the ones who produce wealth. God is. Yes, God uses those who are called to create as his instruments to produce wealth in the world, but he is the one who gives us the ideas, talents, and opportunities to generate financial abundance. In short, "You didn't build that." *He* did, *through* you.

> If God is the one who produces profits through me, then he owns it all, and I am just a steward of the wealth he has entrusted me with.

If we believe we are responsible for our success—that we are the ones who produce wealth—then it is perfectly logical to see profit as a means of rewarding ourselves. If I produce the profits, I own the profits, and thus am free to spend them however I choose, whether that's buying a yacht, traveling the world, or cashing in for an early retirement. But if God is the one who produces profits through me, then he owns it all, and I am just a steward of the wealth he has entrusted me with.

Conduits for Abundance

When Ben Robbins asked me to take over the company he cofounded (Threshold 360) as its first outside CEO, I was honored. I was also eager to learn from Robbins, who lives a lifestyle that is starkly different from any entrepreneur I know. Reading through his impressive résumé, you might expect Robbins to live in a mansion with his wife and two kids. Instead, they live in a tiny home in the inner city where they spend a considerable amount of time and money serving the poor.

Sitting over breakfast, Robbins helped me understand his lifestyle and how he thinks about profit by comparing himself and other Christian entrepreneurs to first-century fishermen such as Peter, Andrew, James, and John, four of Jesus's disciples. "In first-century Palestine, fishing represented a way of providing for your family and your community that was symbiotic with creation," Robbins said. "It was providence manifested. You would show up, and you would simply float along in this reality that you cannot take credit for and abundance would just flow your way. You would bring the fish back and you would offer them to your community and they would be thankful to you, but ultimately to God, since you couldn't take credit for your success. In my work today, God is my collaborator. I can't take credit for the profits my ventures produce. So, are these fish mine? Not really. I am the person who connects the fish from the sea to the village. I am a steward. Entrepreneurs are the conduits for abundance, but it's an abundance that's not ours at all. The idea of 'giving back' is crap."

Any entrepreneur who has raised capital will tell you that a business takes on a different dynamic once you've brought on investors. When we raised capital for Citizinvestor in 2013, we experienced this firsthand. Like most entrepreneurs, we raised our seed round of $150,000 from friends and family. Once the money was in our bank account, my partner and I started operating the business differently, meticulously watching how we spent every dime of our precious investment. The last thing we wanted was to be poor stewards of the investment we had been entrusted with, especially because it was from those we loved most. While this added pressure to our work, I was grateful for the opportunity to catch a glimpse of how I think God wants us to consider the wealth he has entrusted us with. Ultimately, God is the one who gives us everything we need to produce profits through our ventures. He owns everything. Thus, when our entrepreneurial endeavors are blessed with abundance, we don't have the luxury of spending those profits however we see fit. We are stewards, trusted by the One who has called us to create to spend his resources in ways that will honor him.

> Entrepreneurs are the conduits for abundance.

What does God have to say about how we are to spend the abundance he entrusts us with? Quite a lot. Money is the subject of nearly half of Jesus's parables recorded in Scripture. One-seventh of the verses in the New Testament deal with this topic.[3] There is not enough room in these pages to record all the Bible has to say on money, but Jesus's words recorded in Matthew 6:19–21 provide us with a good summary:

Do not store up for yourselves treasures on earth, where moth and rust destroy, and where thieves break in and steal. But store up for yourselves treasures in heaven, where neither moth nor rust destroys, and where thieves do not break in or steal; for where your treasure is, there your heart will be also. (NASB)

The issue of money is an issue of the heart. If our hearts have truly been transformed by the gospel of Jesus Christ, it will radically change the way we think about abundance personally and within our businesses. As pastor Timothy Keller puts it:

If people are materialistic and ungenerous, it means they have not truly understood how Jesus, though rich, became poor for them. It means they have not understood what it means that in Christ we have all riches and treasures. They may subscribe to this as a doctrine, but the affections of their hearts are clinging to material things, finding them more excellent and beautiful than Jesus himself.[4]

We have been called to create by a generous God. A God who created us and all that is around us not out of necessity but out of generosity. A God who, "while we were still sinners," gave his only Son to die in our place so that we might spend eternity with him. If we are to reflect our Creator, we must look at the purpose of profit through the lens of his generous character. As I've discussed this topic with dozens of Christian entrepreneurs, I've observed three primary ways in which we who are called to create can think about the multifaceted purpose of profit: we can give profits away, we can reinvest profits into our own ventures, or we can invest profits in others who are following God's call to create.

Give Profits Away

The daughter of one of the wealthiest men in Taiwan, Cher Wang has never known a life without extreme abundance. After attending school in the United States, Wang began to build her own empire, most notably founding HTC Corporation, which at one point made one in every six smartphones sold in the United States.[5] Today, Wang is one of the wealthiest women in Taiwan and one of the most powerful women in the world.[6] But few know her name. That's because Wang has chosen a simple and humble lifestyle that is in stark

> If we are to reflect our Creator, we must look at profit through the lens of his generous character.

contrast to what we are used to seeing in a technology industry full of celebrity CEOs. She shies away from the trappings of wealth, getting around Taipei and San Francisco in taxis and flying discount carrier Southwest Airlines. When she's not wearing athletic attire outside the office, Wang chooses a uniform of simple black suits.[7]

Wang's Christian faith strongly influences her lifestyle and equips her to view her wealth as a gift from God.[8] For the past few years, Wang's personal wealth has seen a series of ups and downs that correspond to the roller-coaster ride HTC has taken in the ever-changing smartphone market. Wang said, "[God] has let me experience a little bit of blessings at first, then gave me some trials and tribulations, and then let me experience his miraculous guidance and works."[9] But even through drastic changes in personal wealth, Wang has chosen to be a conduit for abundance, giving away substantial portions of the profits she has derived from HTC and her previous ventures. In 2008, Wang donated more than sixty million dollars to finance her church's move into Taipei's Dazhi District. In 2014, when HTC's stock was worth just eighteen percent of what it was worth in 2008,[10] Wang was still giving generously, donating more than twenty-two million dollars to purchase real estate for another evangelical church in Taiwan.[11]

God has used Wang to produce incredible abundance. But because of her faith, Wang doesn't see these profits as a tool for glorifying herself; rather, she views them as an opportunity to glorify God and love others.

Alan Barnhart shares Wang's view on the purpose of profit. In 1986, Barnhart was planning on launching a crane and rigging business with his brother in Memphis, Tennessee, when he pulled out his Bible to see what God had to say about the profits he hoped to make. Not surprisingly, Barnhart found no shortage of verses on the topic of money. He read warnings such as "The love of money is a root of all kinds of evil," "Do not lay up for yourselves treasures on earth," and "It is hard for a rich man to enter the kingdom of heaven."[12]

"I read all these verses, and I thought: 'I want to be good in business, and I'm competitive,'" Barnhart said. "But I didn't want to make a lot of money if doing so would damage my life. And I could see where it really could."[13]

Barnhart saw how money, while not inherently bad, could become idolatrous. That's when he and his brother did something radical, committing to cap their income, ensuring they never made more money than their middle-class neighbors. Instead of spending profits on themselves, they would give most of it away. In their first year in business, the brothers gave away fifty thousand dollars—more than Alan's salary.

This was not a vow to live a life of poverty, though. Barnhart said, "We had vehicles and air conditioning. It was not a Mother Teresa lifestyle." But the Barnharts' decision was a radical one nonetheless, bucking worldly wisdom that tells entrepreneurs that the purpose of profit is to glorify themselves.

For decades, the Barnharts have remained committed to a modest standard of living, marginally increasing their salaries over time to accommodate inflation in the economy and their households (the brothers have eleven children between the two of them). Over the years, their business has been blessed immensely, and the Barnharts have used the company's profits to bless others, donating more than one hundred million dollars to organizations such as Hope International abroad and Citizens for Community Values, which helps women in their own area escape the sex trade.

But in 2006, the Barnhart brothers did something even more radical: they gave their entire $250 million company away. While the Barnharts still run and operate Barnhart Crane & Rigging, the company is now 100 percent owned by the National Christian Foundation, ensuring that the brothers will never see hundreds of millions of dollars in their personal bank accounts.

"That's one of the things that make Alan and Eric so rare: they decided to give it all away," says David Willis, president of the National Christian Foundation. "That was their wealth. They didn't have three other companies. That was it. They actually don't believe that they own their company anyway. It wasn't theirs; it was God's. They were just taking care of it for him. When they gave away their company, it didn't change their life at all. It significantly changed their balance sheet, but it didn't change their lives."[14]

The examples of Wang's and the Barnhart brothers' generosity are inspiring. But too often, I'm afraid that we as Christian entrepreneurs think that the *only* purpose of profit is giving it away. This can lead to unbiblical thinking that the only people doing "real ministry" are the missionaries, churches, and nonprofits we donate money to. As we have already explored, nothing could be further from the truth. If we think the only purpose of profit is to give it away, then we will miss tremendous opportunities to do ministry through our own ventures. The Barnharts get this, reinvesting roughly fifty percent of the company's profits back into their business while giving the other fifty percent away. One of Barnhart Crane and Rigging's core values is "Profit with a Purpose," which in their words means "investing profit to expand the company and to meet the needs of people (physically, mentally, spiritually)."[15] This view of profit—reinvesting it to expand a company and invest in its people—is reminiscent of another Christian entrepreneur whose story we have already touched on: Arthur Guinness.

Reinvest Profits into Our Ventures

On a beautiful Irish-green lawn outside of St. Patrick's Cathedral in Dublin stands a statue of Benjamin Guinness, the grandson of the brewery's founder. The statue serves as a means of recognizing the man who, in 1860, personally funded the restoration of the historic cathedral at an expense of more than £150,000.[16] At the time, Guinness was the wealthiest man in all of Ireland, thanks to the company his family had built for three generations.[17] The Guinness family was known for their generosity, but this project had particular significance for Benjamin Guinness, at least in part because the church played such a significant role in the life of his grandfather Arthur.

As we have already seen, Arthur Guinness was a devout Christian. One Sunday morning, he had the thrill of hearing one of his spiritual heroes preach from the pulpit of St. Patrick's Cathedral, Guinness's home church. The man was John Wesley, the great theologian who, with his brother Charles and contemporary George Whitefield, is credited for founding the evangelical movement that spawned the Methodist church. We don't know exactly what Wesley preached that Sunday morning, but around this time, he was teaching a message that had direct application for entrepreneurs such as Guinness. "Earn all you can. Save all you can. Give all you can," Wesley would say. "Your wealth is evidence of a calling from God, so use your abundance for the good of mankind."[18] Guinness took Wesley's words to heart, allowing the gospel to shape how he and subsequent generations of Guinness owners thought about the purpose of profit. And while the Guinness family was well known for giving away significant amounts of money, they are perhaps best known for reinvesting profits into their business and, in particular, their people. As Stephen Mansfield, author of *The Search for God and Guinness*, points out:

> [Arthur Guinness] was unusual in that he absorbed Wesley's social teaching very deeply and lived it out more radically than most. He took care of the poor, started hospitals and ran his company in a way that was radical—paying twenty percent more for salaries than most other people and providing benefits to his employees that would challenge the accomplishments of Microsoft and Google today.

If you had worked for Guinness in 1928, a year before the Great Depression, you would have had twenty-four-hour medical care, twenty-four-hour dental care, on-site massage therapy. You would have had a savings and loan to help you own a house. Your funeral expenses would have been paid. Your pension would have been paid without you having to make any contributions. The education of your children would have been paid for and maybe your education as well. Your wife would have been given courses and training and benefits of every kind to make a better home.

One of the most moving parts of researching [*The Search for God and Guinness*] was going to Ireland and talking to taxi drivers, talking to professors at Trinity College Dublin, whose lives have been transformed because Guinness intervened and sent the father off to college. Now the son of that father who had gone to college has turned into a college professor.[19]

Arthur Guinness is one of the most successful Christian entrepreneurs of all time. But he didn't see the abundance the business created as something to be hoarded. Changed by the gospel, Guinness saw profit as a means of loving his neighbor as himself, particularly his neighbors who spent their time working at his brewery. "Guinness believed it was what a righteous people would do, what God wanted them to do."[20]

Operating an entrepreneurial endeavor based on the principles we have been exploring in this book is costly, requiring that we reinvest some profits back into our ventures. For Chick-fil-A, this means investing in higher quality ingredients to reflect God's character of excellence. For Grace Harbor Group, this means paying their laundromat managers higher wages and asking them to spend valuable time investing in the lives of their customers. For Embrace Home Loans, this means going above and beyond typical corporate perks and investing in the "whole person." There are countless ways in which our ventures carry out the Lord's will. Thus, while giving profits away to outside organizations is certainly one purpose of profit, reinvesting profits back into our own ventures can be an equally God-honoring way to steward the abundance he has entrusted us with.

Invest Profits in Others Who Are Called to Create

"Jason, no one on our side is going to talk until we hear you hang up." There was an awkward silence on the conference call as the Goldman Sachs team tried to formulate a response to David Morken's sudden demand. Morken, CEO and co-founder of Bandwidth.com, was dialed in to a call with the Goldman Sachs team to discuss plans for Bandwidth.com to raise outside capital. Morken reiterated, "We will wait to continue until I hear that you have dropped off the line. I need to hear a click."[21]

Jason, the Goldman Sachs banker Morken had kicked off the line, had dialed in to the conference call on his own wedding day. Once the groom had hung up, Morken reminded the rest of the Goldman Sachs team that Bandwidth.com "will not pursue funding in a way that obfuscates who we are."

Since the company's founding in 1999, Morken and his business partner and best friend, Henry Kaestner, have been crystal clear about their values and that of their company: "faith, family, work, and fitness, in that order." Kaestner said, "From our earliest meetings, David told me 'My faith is really important to me,' to which I responded 'Me too.' He looked at me intensely again and said 'My faith is really, really important to me.' I responded again, 'Me too.' Finally, he said, 'But I'm a Jesus Freak who has spoken in tongues.' A new Christian, I had no clue what he was talking about, but what was clear to me was his need for me to understand the depths of his faith."[22]

Morken and Kaestner were on the same page: their faith in Jesus Christ was the single most important thing in their lives. It was why they created: to bring glory to the First Entrepreneur and to serve others. But as Morken and Kaestner learned while raising capital for Bandwidth.com in 2001, while most serious investors eventually ask, "Why do you do what you do?" almost none of them understand the answer "To glorify God." The Bandwidth.com founders had several promising first meetings with Silicon Valley venture capital funds. Often, those initial meetings led to second and third meetings, with a few investors flying out to North Carolina to meet with the team at Bandwidth.com's offices. During these more intimate meetings, Morken and Kaestner wanted to be forthcoming on their answer to the "why" question. Kaestner said, "We were bringing on a partner who would be strapped to the mast with us, in the fight with us, so it was important that they knew who we are." These conversations usually took place outside of formal pitch meetings, over casual dinners where the two parties could connect more personally. But inevitably, once the Bandwidth.com founders had laid out their motivations for creating, they were met with blank stares and talks of investment stopped. During this time, Morken and Kaestner met with forty investors, none of whom chose to invest in Bandwidth.com. "This wasn't like we got term sheets we couldn't get along with," Morken said. "This was a complete whiff."[23]

Even without institutional capital, Bandwidth.com has been a tremendous success. Today, the company generates $250 million in annual revenue providing telecommunications services to more than six thousand businesses including Google, Skype, and Vonage. It also owns Republic Wireless, a telecommunications operator with a Wi-Fi–enabled mobile service with more than 250,000 subscribers.

With Bandwidth.com's success, Kaestner saw a purpose of profit separate from giving it away or reinvesting it into his own company. Given his and Morken's difficulty finding likeminded investors a decade earlier, Kaestner launched his own venture capital fund where Christian founders would be free to articulate their "why" with investors who shared their values.

"Institutional capital doesn't know what to make of faith in the workplace, and as a result, there are very real pressures for entrepreneurs to repress their spirituality—to compartmentalize it in order to please investors," Kaestner said. "There are over five thousand venture capital and private equity funds out there, but none of them has the premise of getting behind and investing in Christian-led companies."[24]

When evaluating investment opportunities, Kaestner and his partners look first for solid businesses that any other venture capital fund would be interested in investing in. Their portfolio is made up of companies from the healthcare, IT, and consumer products and services industries, not necessarily "social enterprises." But given the faith of Kaestner and his partners, they are looking for more than a solid return on their investment. They are looking to invest in the lives of other Christian entrepreneurs. As Kaestner shares, "We wanted to create a fund that would come alongside Christ-following entrepreneurs, to help them grow their businesses. But we also wanted to be able to ask questions, not in a prescriptive way, but to discuss questions like, 'When is it appropriate for us to pray with non-believing employees?' and 'Should we hire a corporate chaplain or not?' Things like that. There's something powerful about investing in Christian-led companies."[25]

The name of Kaestner's fund? Sovereign's Capital. A not-so-subtle reminder to Kaestner and the world of who owns financial abundance in the first place.

The purpose of profit is not as simple as giving it all away. There are many ways in which God calls us to steward the abundance he blesses us with through our ventures. There is not a one-size-fits-all answer to what you are to do with the profits you have been blessed with. But if we understand that it is God, not us, who produces wealth, and if we grasp the generosity we have been shown in Christ, we will not see profits as a means of glorifying ourselves; instead, we will view our abundance as an opportunity to glorify God and love others.

12

creating for the kingdom

Throughout this book, we have been exploring how following the voice of our Caller shapes our creating today. In part 1, we learned that God was the First Entrepreneur, and that when we create we are doing so much more than developing products; we are reflecting the character of our Father. We dispelled the pervasive myth that work is inherently bad and meaningless with the biblical view of work as an inherently good act of worship, thus removing any sort of secular/spiritual hierarchy of callings. And we bucked the world's self-centric questions for evaluating career opportunities, asking a different set of others-oriented questions to discern our call to create.

In part 2, we explored how our calling shapes the why, what, and how of our creating. We examined our motivations for creating, choosing not to create to make a name for ourselves but to reveal God's character and love others. We looked at how those priorities shape the products we choose

205

to make. And we examined what it looks like to holistically integrate the gospel into our ventures, beginning with striving for excellence in everything we do and prioritizing people over profit.

In part 3, we walked through a series of challenges that are unique or especially acute for those who are called to create. We wrestled with the tension between trusting and hustling and how we as driven entrepreneurs can find true rest. We thought deeply about how we might respond differently to failure to show the hope we have in Christ. And we learned about the challenge of continually renewing our minds through regular communion with God, our partners, and other believers.

In this fourth and final part of the book, we have been exploring "the bottom line" for our ventures, beginning with a look at how our entrepreneurial endeavors can be powerful vehicles for fulfilling our command to create disciples, and then moving into an analysis of the purpose of profit. Each of these topics significantly impacts our creating today, challenging us to reimagine our work as service to the One who has called us to create. But the question we've been building to is this: While our creating clearly matters for this life, does it really matter for eternity?

An Entrepreneur and a Theologian

Hordes of Silicon Valley entrepreneurs rushed to find open seats in the auditorium, eager to hear from one of their greatest heroes, Peter Thiel. In 1998, Thiel cofounded PayPal, serving as the company's CEO through their IPO in 2002. Following this entrepreneurial success, Thiel began making investments in early-stage companies that paid off big, including making the first outside investment in Facebook in 2004. Over the past decade, Thiel's stature as a leading thinker and doer in Silicon Valley has risen dramatically, culminating most recently with his #1 *New York Times* bestselling book, *Zero to One*.

The fact that a group of young, hipster techies were clamoring to grab a seat for a Thiel talk is not surprising. But what made this event so remarkable was that Thiel was there to discuss the Christian faith. While Thiel is well-known for his success as an entrepreneur and investor, few people know that he is a professing Christian, hence at least some of the allure that had driven these entrepreneurs to hear him discuss his faith in Northern California where, as HBO's *Silicon Valley* says, "Christianity is borderline illegal."

To make the event even more intriguing, Thiel was joined onstage by N. T. Wright. If you recognize the names of both Thiel and Wright, congratulations, you are in what has to be an infinitesimally small cross-section of people who are familiar with both the work of one of the world's most successful entrepreneurs and investors (Thiel), and one of the world's leading Christian theologians (Wright).[1]

Their ninety-minute discussion ranged from topics such as whether or not humans can end death to how entrepreneurs can help solve poverty. But what I found most interesting was a discussion on whether or not science and technological progress are at odds with faith, as is so often portrayed in culture with Christians (often rightfully) earning the reputation as being "critics, consumers, copiers, condemners of culture."[2]

Thiel weighed in, saying, "I grew up as an evangelical Christian. There certainly is a sense in which scientific technological utopia seems quite at odds with a Christian worldview, but I think there are some commonalities that are worth stressing. One very important commonality is that both have this view that the future will look very different from the present or the past. This is certainly the view that is presented in science fiction, it's presented in the New Jerusalem."[3] In a separate forum, Thiel put it this way: "Insofar as Christians don't just hope for a better world but also hear a call to be active partners in the fulfillment of that hope, I think building new and better tools is one way to do that."[4]

What in the world is Thiel talking about? He is articulating a biblically sound view of heaven that has tragically been lost in much of the modern church: that earth *is not* "heaven's waiting room" but rather the place that God has created us to dwell in forever.

If this all sounds very foreign to you, stay with me for a minute. I was in your shoes for the first two decades of my life as a Christian. Growing up, I believed that when I died or when Christ returned, I would be taken up into the clouds to live forever in some hybrid church service/retirement home where there would be no work, no creating, and certainly no looking back to earth. Unfortunately, this is often the only heaven portrayed in the church today. I love how pastor John Mark Comer describes this theology in his excellent book *Garden City*: "This is essentially a theology of evacuation. The sentiment is, Let's get out of *here* [earth] and go somewhere *else*."[5] To be honest, the thought of this used to really depress me. Something in my soul feels a deep connection to earth. Something in my soul feels like I was called to create forever. Something in my soul tells me that the American caricature of heaven simply can't be all there is to eternity.

That something in my soul was really Someone: the Holy Spirit, pointing me to the Bible, where God has graciously revealed a much more awe-inspiring and invigorating picture of what he has planned for our eternal existence.

To be clear, the "theology of evacuation" isn't all wrong. The Bible promises believers of Jesus Christ that we "will be with [Him] in paradise" (Luke 23:43) the moment we breathe our last breath in this life. That paradise obviously isn't on this earth. In his exceptional book *Heaven*, Randy Alcorn refers to this destination as "Intermediate (or Present) Heaven."[6] This is the heaven we grew up learning about in Sunday school. But intermediate heaven is only half the story. Throughout the New Testament, Jesus and his disciples often refer to death as "sleep," a temporary state until Jesus comes back to resurrect our physical bodies and renew the earth. John gives us a prophetic glimpse of this in Revelation:

> Then I saw a new heaven and a new earth; for the first heaven and the first earth passed away, and there is no longer any sea. And I saw the holy city, new Jerusalem, coming down out of heaven from God, made ready as a bride adorned for her husband. And I heard a loud voice from the throne, saying, "Behold, the tabernacle of God is among men, and He will dwell among them, and they shall be His people, and God Himself will be among them, and He will wipe away every tear from their eyes; and there will no longer be any death; there will no longer be any mourning, or crying, or pain; the first things have passed away." (Rev. 21:1–4 NASB)

In other words, earth *is not* "our temporary home"[7] but where we will dwell with God forever—not the cursed earth we inhabit today but a new earth totally redeemed by its Creator. Alcorn illustrates this eloquently:

> Suppose you live in a homeless shelter in Miami. One day you inherit a beautiful house in Santa Barbara, California, fully furnished, on a gorgeous hillside overlooking the ocean. With the home comes a wonderful job doing something you've always wanted to do. Not only that, but you'll also be near close family members who moved from Miami many years ago.
>
> On your flight to Santa Barbara, you'll change planes in Denver, where you'll spend an afternoon. Some other family members, whom you haven't seen in years, will meet you at the Denver airport and board the plane with you to Santa Barbara, where they have inherited their own beautiful houses on another part of the same vast estate. Naturally, you look forward to seeing them. Now, when the Miami ticket agent asks you, "Where are you headed?" would you say, "Denver"? No. You would say, "Santa Barbara," because that's your final destination. If you mentioned Denver at all, you would say, "I'm going to Santa Barbara *by way of* Denver."
>
> When you talk to your friends in Miami about where you're going to live, would you focus on Denver? No. You might not even mention Denver, even though you will be a Denver-dweller for several hours. Even if you left the airport and spent a day or a week in Denver, it still wouldn't be your focus. Denver is just a stop along the way. Your true destination—your new long-term home—is in Santa Barbara.
>
> Similarly, the Heaven we will go to when we die, the intermediate Heaven, is a temporary dwelling place. It's a wonderfully nice place (much better than the Denver airport!), but it's still a stop along the way to our final destination: the New Earth.[8]

The Reversal of Babel

Great, so hopefully we have cleared up one of the greatest misunderstandings of Scripture in our time, but we still haven't answered the question I posed earlier in this chapter: While our creating clearly matters for this life, does it really matter for eternity? In one of the richest passages of Scripture on the topic of eternity, the apostle Paul spends fifty-eight verses in 1 Corinthians 15 expounding upon heaven and our coming bodily resurrection. You may expect

> Earth is not "our temporary home" but where we will dwell with God forever.

him to end this exposition by saying something to the effect of, "Since it's all going to 'burn up' anyway, what you do in this life doesn't really matter." But that's not at all what Paul says. Instead, Paul uses his last words in the chapter to encourage us to "be steadfast . . . in the work of the Lord, knowing that your toil is not in vain in the Lord" (1 Cor. 15:58 NASB). Now, "the work of the Lord" almost certainly refers to overtly evangelical work: sharing the gospel, serving the poor, working to strengthen the local church, and so forth. But Paul doesn't exclude other types of work, including our work as entrepreneurs and creators, and I bet that's on purpose. Commenting on this passage, N. T. Wright, the theologian who joined Thiel onstage in Silicon Valley, says this:

> What you do in the present—by painting, preaching, singing, sewing, praying, teaching, building hospitals, digging wells, campaigning for justice, writing poems, caring for the needy, loving your neighbor as yourself—will last into God's future. These activities are not simply ways of making the present life a little less beastly, a little more bearable, until the day

when we leave it behind altogether. They are part of what we may call building for God's kingdom.[9]

One of the most prophetic passages on the new earth is found in Isaiah 60. The prophet writes:

> Arise, shine, for your light has come,
>   and the glory of the LORD rises upon you.
> See, darkness covers the earth
>   and thick darkness is over the peoples,
> but the LORD rises upon you
>   and his glory appears over you.
> Nations will come to your light,
>   and kings to the brightness of your dawn.
>
> Lift up your eyes and look about you:
>   All assemble and come to you;
> your sons come from afar,
>   and your daughters are carried on the hip.
> Then you will look and be radiant,
>   your heart will throb and swell with joy;
> the wealth on the seas will be brought to you,
>   to you the riches of the nations will come.
> Herds of camels will cover your land,
>   young camels of Midian and Ephah.
> And all from Sheba will come,
>   bearing gold and incense
>   and proclaiming the praise of the LORD.
> All Kedar's flocks will be gathered to you,
>   the rams of Nebaioth will serve you;
> they will be accepted as offerings on my altar,
>   and I will adorn my glorious temple.
>
> Who are these that fly along like clouds,
>   like doves to their nests?

Surely the islands look to me;
    in the lead are the ships of Tarshish,
bringing your children from afar,
    with their silver and gold,
to the honor of the LORD your God,
    the Holy One of Israel,
      for he has endowed you with splendor.

Foreigners will rebuild your walls,
    and their kings will serve you.
Though in anger I struck you,
    in favor I will show you compassion.
Your gates will always stand open,
    they will never be shut, day or night,
so that people may bring you the wealth of the
      nations—
    their kings led in triumphal procession.
For the nation or kingdom that will not serve you
      will perish;
    it will be utterly ruined.

The glory of Lebanon will come to you,
    the juniper, the fir and the cypress together,
to adorn my sanctuary;
    and I will glorify the place for my feet.
The children of your oppressors will come bowing
      before you;
    all who despise you will bow down at your feet
and will call you the City of the LORD,
    Zion of the Holy One of Israel. (Isa. 60:1–14)

What is happening in this scene? This is a reversal of the events that surrounded the Tower of Babel. As you recall from chapter 4, the Babylonians had discovered the technical innovation of brickmaking. But with this invention came the temptation to use the new technology to glorify themselves rather than God. "They said, 'Come, let us build ourselves a city, with a tower that reaches to the heavens, so that we may make a name for ourselves; otherwise we will be scattered over the face of the whole earth'" (Gen. 11:4). But the Babylonians' attempt to rob God of the glory due him alone earned them the thing they dreaded most: God "scattered them from there over all the earth, and they stopped building the city" (v. 8).

Now, Isaiah is sharing a prophetic vision of the reversal of Babel, of all the nations coming back together into "the city of the Lord." Isaiah is seeing a vision similar to John's in Revelation of the New Jerusalem, where God will reign forever on the new earth. But unlike in Babel, the people are not using their creations to glorify themselves; they are laying their creations down as an offering at the feet of the First Entrepreneur. The people of Tarshish bring their ships, Midian and Ephah bring their livestock, Sheba brings gold and frankincense. "The wealth of the nations," the best creations of the nations, are being brought into the eternal city to glorify the One who called the people to create.

> Just as God called us to be co-creators with him in Eden, he is graciously calling us to co-create with him for the new earth.

I'm afraid many who are called to create view heaven as a place without culture, void of anything we might create in this life. That is simply not what the Bible teaches. Scripture tells us that, at a minimum, there will be cities, gates, rivers, houses, food, vineyards, fruit, roads, and music on the new earth. In short, there will be culture, the product of our creations. The Bible makes it clear that we will work without the curse forever on the new earth; I think it's safe to assume that those of us who are called to create will use our entrepreneurial skills to create as an act of worship. But Isaiah shows us that it's not just the things we create in heaven that will last for eternity; what we create *today* has the potential to live on forever on the new earth. While God clearly points to people as the crown jewel of creation, giving extra weight to the way we love and serve people as we build our ventures, he also deems the products of our creations worthy of eternal consideration. Just as God called us to be co-creators with him in the Garden of Eden, he is graciously calling us to co-create with him on the new earth. In the words of Andy Crouch:

> The city [New Jerusalem] is already a cultural artifact, the work of a master Architect and Artist. The citizens themselves are the redeemed people of the Lamb, drawn from "every tribe and language and people and nation" (Rev. 5:9). But God's handiwork, artifacts and people alike, are not all that is found in the city. Also in the city are "the glory and the honor of the nations"—brought into the city by none other than "the kings of the earth." So it's a fascinating exercise to ask about any cultural artifact: can we imagine this making it into the new Jerusalem?[10]

And *that* is the question I want to leave you with as we wrap up this book. Can you imagine your creations, the products of your entrepreneurial endeavors, passing through into eternity? Are you creating in such a way that our Lord will view your work as an offering of worship? Can you see the

First Entrepreneur taking your creations and working them into his eternal masterpiece? If we reimagine our creating as a means not of glorifying ourselves but of glorifying God and loving others as we have been exploring in this book, I think we have a shot.

On the new earth, our homes may be decorated with paintings from Kristin Joy Taylor, or we may find Bible verses hand-lettered by Krystal Whitten adorning our walls. Maybe we will join the employees of Chick-fil-A and In-N-Out for a feast of exceptional chicken sandwiches and burgers. Who knows, God may even choose to allow a Guinness or two to pass through heaven's gates. There won't be a need to tell time, but maybe Casper ten Boom's watches will meet us on the other side so that we may wonder at the marvelous creation of the timepiece and remember how they were used to protect God's people. It's hard to imagine eternity without Bach's Cello Suite No. 1 in G Major, played *Soli Deo Gloria*. With perfect, redeemed bodies, there may not be a need for Joel Ohman's Exercise.com apps, but if God deems exercise an act of worship, maybe even Ohman's product will be a part of our eternal existence. We don't know what the dress code will be on the new earth, but after our workout we might need some clean clothes, and the team at Grace Harbor Group may be there to serve us much like they serve the poor through their business today. Maybe the New Jerusalem's library will be filled with books authored by C. S. Lewis, J. R. R. Tolkien, and Hannah Brencher. I pray even this book will be considered among "the glory and the honor of the nations." Instead of teaching children how to capture their perspective of poverty, maybe Angela Popplewell's curriculum at 100cameras will be used to teach us all how to capture a glimpse of God's glory using HTC smartphones developed by Cher Wang. Our children may be wrapped up in EllieFunDay blankets, their feet covered in TOMS Shoes. And we'll almost certainly sing "It is well with my soul," because, in fact, it will be—forever.

If the prospect of your products being included on the new earth doesn't motivate you to create for your Caller, I don't know what will. I love Wright's idea of "building *for* God's kingdom." We human beings do not build the kingdom. Only God does that. But all of us have the opportunity to create *for* the kingdom, laying our work products down at the feet of the First Entrepreneur, who just might choose to take our raw materials and work them into his final creation.

So, as we close this book, I pray that you and I will create for the kingdom. If our creations are to be considered "the glory and the honor of the nations," they must be excellent for sure. But I think creating for the kingdom means more than creating excellent end-products. It means deeply integrating the gospel into how we create, prioritizing people over profit, using our organizations to make disciples, and creating in line with the other challenging truths we have already explored in this book. It's about choosing the path of the entrepreneur and creator not primarily so that we can "work for ourselves," set our own hours, control our own destiny, or make a name for ourselves. We choose this path because Someone has called us to create. We choose this path because God gave us the passion, giftings, and opportunities to use our entrepreneurial talents

> All of us have the opportunity to create for the kingdom, laying our work products down at the feet of the First Entrepreneur.

to glorify him, love others, and create something that has a shot at being considered the glory of the nations. So my final charge to you and to myself is this: create in a way that our work can never be confused as a mere "job." Create in a way that clearly conveys to ourselves and the world that we work sacrificially for someone else. We work for the One who has called us to create.

acknowledgments

While there are at least a hundred people who helped shape this book, a few deserve special acknowledgment and thanks.

To Kara, my loving wife and closest confidant: Thank you for encouraging me to follow my calling, even when it meant writing a book and running a company while raising two kids under the age of two. You continue to be the best picture of grace I have ever seen.

To my startup spouse, Tony: Thank you for encouraging me to write this book when it was no more than "an interesting idea for a blog post" about the First Entrepreneur. I treasure your friendship and partnership.

To my agent, D. J. Snell: Thank you for believing in me and this project and for your patience with an overeager entrepreneur-turned-writer. You are exceptional at your craft.

To Brian Thomasson: Thank you for taking a risk on me and this project. I will never forget the faith you placed in me and this message.

To the rest of the team at Baker Books (and Nicci Jordan Hubert): Thank you for your openness to new ideas and for making this book the best product it could be.

To those I interviewed for this book: Thank you for being so accessible and transparent. Without your inspirational stories, this book quite literally would not exist.

To Timothy Keller, Andy Crouch, C. S. Lewis, John Mark Comer, Randy Alcorn, and N. T. Wright: Thank you for helping me love Jesus more and for laying the theological foundations for this book.

To Chris Basham, Clay Brown, and Dr. Benjamin Quinn: Thank you for serving as my "theological sounding board."

To those who read advance copies of this book, and my many friends who graciously discussed these topics over countless dinners and coffee: Thank you for shaping the ideas of *Called to Create*.

To Chris Perry and Ashley Penny: Thank you for helping me build a community of Christian entrepreneurs and creatives. Without you, this book would have a much smaller audience.

To the Called to Create photographers (calledtocreate .org/photographers): Thank you for contributing your God-given gifts to create the look and feel of @CalledToCreate.

To the Called to Create Launch Team (calledtocreate.org/launchteam): Any success this book experiences is in large part due to you sharing this message with the world. Thank you!

To Stewart, Dennis, Wade, and Rick: Thank you for your mentorship and for allowing me to observe what it looks like to follow the call to create well.

To my dad: Thank you for loving and ministering to people through your business. You are an inspiration.

To the growing Called to Create community: Thank you for continuing to inspire me with the way you glorify God and love others through your creating.

Finally, to the One who called me to create: Thank you for the gift of entrepreneurship and creativity. Thank you for calling us to co-create with you.

about the author

Jordan Raynor is a serial entrepreneur and bestselling author who leads a growing community of Christians following God's call to create. He is the founder of Vocreo, where his team helps entrepreneurs across a wide range of industries launch and grow their businesses. In 2016, Jordan took an indefinite leave of absence from Vocreo to take on the role of CEO at one of the firm's portfolio companies: the venture-backed tech startup Threshold 360. Jordan is also a cofounder of Citizinvestor, the largest crowdfunding platform for government projects in the United States.

In 2011, Jordan's first company was acquired by Engage, deemed a "mega-interactive agency" by Mashable. At Engage, Jordan's team led digital strategy for some of the most high-profile political and consumer brands in the world, including Paul Ryan, Newt Gingrich, Google, Foursquare, and Walmart.

A highly sought-after public speaker on the topic of entrepreneurship, Jordan has spoken at Harvard University, SXSW, TEDx, the World Forum for Democracy, the *Guardian*'s

Activate Summit, and many other events around the world. Jordan has twice been selected as a Google Fellow and served in the Bush White House in 2006. He is a sixth-generation Floridian currently residing in Tampa with his wife, Kara, and their two young daughters, Ellison and Kate. The Raynors are members of The Church at Odessa.

notes

Introduction

1. For bios and information on how to connect with the entrepreneurs featured in this book, visit calledtocreate.org/stories.

2. Google Ngram Viewer, "Entrepreneurship," https://books.google.com /ngrams/graph?content=entrepreneurship.

3. Dictionary.com, "Entrepreneur," http://dictionary.reference.com/browse /entrepreneur.

4. Ibid.

5. Merriam-Webster, "Entrepreneur," http://www.merriam-webster.com /dictionary/entrepreneurship.

6. To watch this great scene, visit calledtocreate.org/jobs.

Chapter 1 The First Entrepreneur

1. Jerry King, "Why Creativity Matters," speech, 2008, Tampa Covenant Church, Tampa, FL.

2. C. S. Lewis, *The Magician's Nephew* (New York: HarperCollins, 1994), 105.

3. John Piper and Jonathan Edwards, *God's Passion for His Glory: Living the Vision of Jonathan Edwards, with the Complete Text of The End for Which God Created the World.* (Wheaton: Crossway, 1998), 159.

4. No one has influenced my faith and my thinking on this topic more than Dr. Keller. If you haven't binge-read everything he's ever written, start now.

5. Timothy Keller, "Creation & Creativity," speech at Ei Forum, 7 World Trade Center, New York City, April 16, 2010, http://www.gospelinlife.com /sermons/ei-forum-tim-keller-keynote-creation-creativity-8215.

6. Michael Gungor, "Beautiful Things," 2010, https://open.spotify.com /track/06wxyCQFJOT0bjvSPMQj7x.

7. I reference a lot of books throughout *Called to Create*. For a list of my favorite recommendations to help you go deeper in connecting your faith with your work as an entrepreneur, visit calledtocreate.org/bookshelf.

8. Andy Crouch, *Culture Making: Recovering Our Creative Calling* (Downers Grove, IL: InterVarsity Press, 2008), 23.

9. Keller, "Creation & Creativity."

10. Dr. Klaus Issler, "Jesus's Career . . . Before His Ministry," *Institute for Faith, Work, and Economics*, May 7, 2014, https://tifwe.org/jesus-career -before-his-ministry.

11. Ibid.

12. John Piper, "Glorifying God . . . Period," *Desiring God*, July 15, 2013, http://www.desiringgod.org/messages/glorifying-god-period.

13. A baby, baby grand, if you will.

14. John Piper, "Why Did God Create the World?" *Desiring God*, September 22, 2012, http://www.desiringgod.org/messages/why-did-god-create-the-world.

15. Timothy Keller and Katherine Leary Alsdorf, *Every Good Endeavor: Connecting Your Work to God's Work* (New York: Penguin, 2012), 56.

16. Ibid., 48.

17. Keller, "Creation & Creativity."

Chapter 2 The Goodness of Work

1. Crouch, *Culture Making: Recovering Our Creative Calling*, 97.

2. Barna Group, "Christians on Leadership, Calling and Career," *Barna Group*, June 3, 2013, https://www.barna.org/barna-update/culture/609-chris tians-on-leadership-calling-and-career#.Vl2W6d-rRE5.

3. Jena McGregor, "The Average Work Week Is Now 47 Hours," *The Washington Post*, September 2, 2014, https://www.washingtonpost.com/news /on-leadership/wp/2014/09/02/the-average-work-week-is-now-47-hours.

4. Chris Basham, personal email to author. Used by permission.

5. As quoted in Randy C. Alcorn, *Heaven* (Carol Stream, IL: Tyndale, 2004), 397.

6. Dominic Timms, "US Version of The Office Scores Ratings Victory," *The Guardian*, March 29, 2005, http://www.theguardian.com/media/2005 /mar/29/broadcasting.

7. Jeff Van Duzer, *Why Business Matters to God (And What Still Needs to Be Fixed)* (InterVarsity: Downers Grove, IL: 2010), 28–29.

8. Corrie ten Boom, Elizabeth Sherrill, and John L. Sherrill, *The Hiding Place* (Bloomington, MN: Chosen, 2006), 26.

9. Ibid., 20.

10. Ibid., 115–16.

11. Ibid., 168.

12. To see what I mean, take a virtual tour of the street, the watch shop, and the Beje at calledtocreate.org/tenboom.

13. Benjamin T. Quinn and Walter R. Strickland II, *Every Waking Hour: An Introduction to Work and Vocation for Christians* (Bellingham, WA: Lexham Press, 2016), Kindle ed.

14. Lee Hardy, *The Fabric of This World: Inquiries into Calling, Career Choice, and the Design of Human Work* (Grand Rapids: Eerdmans, 1990), 67.

15. Mark Russell, *Work as Worship: How the CEOs of Interstate Batteries, Hobby Lobby, PepsiCo, Tyson Foods and More Bring Meaning to Their Work* (Boise, ID: Elevate, 2012), Kindle loc. 58–59.

Chapter 3 Discerning Our Calling

1. Dorothy L. Sayers, *Letters to a Diminished Church: Passionate Arguments for the Relevance of Christian Doctrine* (Nashville: W. Publishing Group, 2004), 127–28.

2. Kent Hoover, "Entrepreneurship Booms: Record Number of Americans Starting Businesses," *The Business Journals*, September 2, 2015, http://www.bizjournals.com/bizjournals/washingtonbureau/2015/09/entrepreneurship-booms-record-number-of-americans.html.

3. "Overview," Center for Faith and Work, http://www.faithandwork.com/programs/7-entrepreneurship-innovation.

4. For those keeping track, that's two Aaron Sorkin references already. More to come.

5. "'The Social Network' and 12 More Movies That Defined a Generation," *Rolling Stone*, September 30, 2010, http://www.rollingstone.com/movies/pictures/the-social-network-and-12-more-movies-that-defined-a-generation-20100930.

6. Kristin Rawls, "7 Things the Media Missed about the Chick-fil-A Saga," *Alternet*, August 8, 2012, http://www.alternet.org/activism/7-things-media-missed-about-chick-fil-saga.

7. Disclosure: The Sketch Effect is a client of ours at Vocreo.

8. Sayers, "Why Work?" in *Letters to a Diminished Church*, 132.

9. Keller and Alsdorf, *Every Good Endeavor*, 76.

10. "What Luther Didn't Say about Vocation," *Word & World* 25, no. 4 (2005).

11. Crouch, *Culture Making: Recovering Our Creative Calling*, 256.

12. As is writing a book with a newborn in the house. Good (crazy) times!

13. Grace Wong, "Blake Mycoskie: Sole Ambition," *CNN*, September 26, 2008, http://www.cnn.com/2008/BUSINESS/09/26/mycoskie.profile/index.html?eref=rss_latest.

14. Blake Mycoskie, *Start Something That Matters* (New York: Random House, 2011), Kindle loc. 77–79.

15. Ibid., Kindle loc. 58–59.

16. Ibid., Kindle loc. 67–71.

17. Russell, *Work as Worship*, Kindle loc. 1259–60.

18. "Blake Mycoskie at The Global Leadership Summit," YouTube video, posted by wcavideo, April 12, 2012, https://www.youtube.com/watch?v=f5OCcD4qbk8.

19. Mycoskie, *Start Something That Matters*, Kindle loc. 76–77.

20. "About TOMS," TOMS Shoes, http://www.toms.com/corporate-responsibility.

21. Greg Roumeliotis and Olivia Oran, "Exclusive: Bain Capital to Invest in Shoemaker TOMS—Sources," *Reuters*, August 20, 2014, http://www.reuters.com/article/us-toms-baincapital-idUSKBN0GK1ZZ20140820.

22. Lucia Hulsether, "TOMS Shoes and the Spiritual Politics of Neoliberalism," *Religion and Politics*, October 1, 2013, http://religionandpolitics.org/2013/10/01/toms-shoes-and-the-spiritual-politics-of-neoliberalism.

23. To view Mycoskie's full interview at Willow Creek Church, visit calledtocreate.org/toms.

24. "Blake Mycoskie at The Global Leadership Summit," YouTube video.

25. Russell, *Work as Worship*, Kindle loc. 1261–62.

26. Robert A. Sirico, "The Biblical Case for Entrepreneurship," *Religion and Liberty* 11, no. 1, http://www.acton.org/pub/religion-liberty/volume-11-number-1/biblical-case-entrepreneurship.

Chapter 4 Why We Create

1. Patrick Reikofski, "How Many People Go to Disney World Every Day?" *Temporary Tourist*, June 3, 2015, http://temporarytourist.com/how-many-people-go-to-disney-world-every-day.

2. Neal Gabler, *Walt Disney* (New York: Random House, 2006), Kindle loc. 10268–69.

3. David Koenig, *Realityland* (Irvine, CA: Bonaventure Press, 2014), 38–39.

4. Gabler, *Walt Disney*, Kindle loc. 10582–92.

5. John Piper, "The Pride of Babel and the Praise of Christ," *Desiring God*, September 2, 2007, http://www.desiringgod.org/messages/the-pride-of-babel-and-the-praise-of-christ.

6. Calvin Stapert, "To the Glory of God Alone," *Christian History*, 2007, https://www.christianhistoryinstitute.org/magazine/article/to-the-glory-of-god-alone.

7. Ibid.

8. Calvin R. Stapert, "To the Glory of God Alone," *Christian History* 95 (2007), http://www.christianitytoday.com/history/issues/issue-95/to-glory-of-god-alone.html.

9. This is the first of many Easter eggs I have placed in the book for my fellow *Hamilton* fans. Happy hunting!

10. This is one of my favorite songs from my all-time favorite musical. To listen to it, visit calledtocreate.org/hamilton.

Chapter 5 What We Create

1. This speech is really exceptional. To view it in its entirety, visit calledtocreate.org/praxis.

2. "An Alternative Imagination: Dave Blanchard // 2016 Business Accelerator Finale," Vimeo video, posted by *Praxis*, March 23, 2016, https://vimeo.com/160102973.

3. Dave Blanchard, "An Alternative Imagination," *Praxis*, accessed April 17, 2017, http://praxislabs.org/resources/videos.

4. Quinn and Strickland, *Every Waking Hour*, Kindle ed.

5. Crouch, *Culture Making: Recovering Our Creative Calling*, 214.

6. "CS Lewis to be honoured in Poets' Corner," *BBC*, November 22, 2012, http://www.bbc.com/news/entertainment-arts-20426778.

7. C. S. Lewis, *On Stories: And Other Essays on Literature* (Dallas: Harvest Books, 2002), 46.

8. "The Deeper Truth behind the Chronicles of Narnia," *CBN*, http://www.cbn.com/books/deeper-truth-behind-chronicles-narnia.

9. Timothy Keller, *Why God Made Cities*, ebook, accessed April 17, 2017, https://www.redeemercitytocity.com/ebook/.

10. Dan Schawbel, "Scott Harrison: How he Started Charity: Water and What He Learned in the Process," *Forbes*, July 22, 2013, http://www.forbes.com/sites/danschawbel/2013/07/22/scott-harrison-how-he-started-charity-water-and-what-he-learned-in-the-process/#f5af6a17c5e3.

11. "From Nightclub Promoter to Entrepreneur," *Inc.*, December 27, 2012, http://www.inc.com/scott-harrison/from-nightclub-promoter-to-entrepreneur.html.

12. Rachael Chong, "How the Founder of Charity: Water Went from Packing Clubs to Building Wells," *Fast Company*, December 10, 2012, http://www.fastcoexist.com/1681043/how-the-founder-of-charitywater-went-from-packing-clubs-to-building-wells.

13. "Scott's Story," Charity: Water, accessed April 17, 2017, http://www.charitywater.org/about/scotts_story.php.

14. "From Nightclub Promoter to Entrepreneur," *Inc.*, December 27, 2012, http://www.inc.com/scott-harrison/from-nightclub-promoter-to-entrepreneur.html.

15. Chong, "How the Founder of Charity: Water Went from Packing Clubs to Building Wells."

16. "Scott's Story," Charity: Water.
17. "From Nightclub Promoter to Entrepreneur."
18. Chong, "How the Founder of Charity: Water Went from Packing Clubs to Building Wells."
19. "Mission Statement," Charity: Water, accessed April 17, 2017, https ://www.charitywater.org/about.
20. Ibid.
21. Stephen Mansfield, "The Story of God and Guinness," *RELEVANT*, March 24, 2010, http://www.relevantmagazine.com/god/mission/features /20993-god-and-guinness#KdPe15obp6H2K9rX.99.
22. Stephen Mansfield, *The Search for God and Guinness: A Biography of the Beer That Changed the World* (Nashville: Thomas Nelson, 2009), 254–55.

Chapter 6 How We Create

1. Laura Leonard, "Faith, Fashion, and Forever 21," *Christianity Today*, March 2009, http://www.christianitytoday.com/women/2009/march/faith -fashion-and-forever-21.html.
2. Eva Wiseman, "The Gospel according to Forever 21," *The Guardian*, July 16, 2011, http://www.theguardian.com/lifeandstyle/2011/jul/17/forever-21 -fast-fashion-america.
3. Nancy Cleeland, "Lawsuit Against Forever 21 Alleges Unfair Labor Practices," *Los Angeles Times*, September 7, 2001, http://articles.latimes.com /2001/sep/07/business/fi-43072.
4. Jenna Sauers, "How Forever 21 Keeps Getting Away with Designer Knockoffs," *Jezebel*, July 20, 2011, http://jezebel.com/5822762/how-forever -21-keeps-getting-away-with-designer-knockoffs.
5. Dave Blanchard, Steve Graves, and Josh Kwan, *From Concept to Scale* (New York: Praxis Media, 2013), 25.
6. "Corporate," In-N-Out Burger, http://www.in-n-out.com/employment /corporate.aspx.
7. Stacy Perman, *In-N-Out Burger: A Behind-the-Counter Look at the Fast-Food Chain That Breaks All the Rules* (New York: HarperCollins, 2010), 138–39.
8. Ibid.
9. Sayers, *Letters to a Diminished Church*, 132.
10. Robert A. Sirico, *The Entrepreneurial Vocation* (Grand Rapids: Acton, 2001), 7.
11. Andy Stanley, "Better Before Bigger," *Andy Stanley Leadership Podcast*, May 3, 2013, http://feedproxy.google.com/~r/AndyStanleyLeadershipPodcast /~3/JByw0lNuxBM/Better-Before-Bigger-2013.mp3.

12. Chick-fil-A, "Chick-fil-A's New Grilled Recipe, Entrée Lineup Set to 'Transform' Menu," April 7, 2014, http://inside.chick-fil-a.com/new-grilled-recipe-entree-lineup-2014.

13. Truett S. Cathy, *Eat Mor Chikin: Inspire More People* (Decatur, GA: Looking Glass Books, 2002), 193.

14. Ashlee Vance, *Elon Musk: Tesla, SpaceX, and the Quest for a Fantastic Future* (New York: HarperCollins, 2015), 340.

15. King, "Why Creativity Matters."

16. Dale Partridge, *People Over Profit: Break the System, Live with Purpose, Be More Successful* (Nashville: Thomas Nelson, 2015), 73–74.

Chapter 7 Trust, Hustle, and Rest

1. "Our Story," PikToChart, https://piktochart.com/our-story.

2. "About Us," Teach for America, https://www.teachforamerica.org/about-us.

3. Keller and Alsdorf, *Every Good Endeavor*, 236–37.

Chapter 8 Responding to Failure

1. I dug up an archived video of this Startup Funeral that is pretty great. To view it, visit calledtocreate.org/funeral.

2. Shane Snow, *Smartcuts: The Breakthrough Power of Lateral Thinking* (New York: HarperCollins, 2014), 58.

3. Breena Kerr, "Depression Among Entrepreneurs Is an Epidemic Nobody Is Talking About," *The Hustle*, October 26, 2015, http://thehustle.co/depression-among-entrepreneurs-is-an-epidemic-nobody-is-talking-about.

4. Ibid.

5. "The Y Combinator Chronicles," *Fast Company*, http://www.fastcompany.com/section/the-y-combinator-chronicles.

6. John Newton, "Amazing Grace," 1779.

7. Keller and Alsdorf, *Every Good Endeavor*, 220.

8. Erwin Raphael McManus, *The Artisan Soul* (New York: HarperCollins, 2014).

9. Horatio Gates Spafford, "When Peace Like a River," 1873.

10. Ibid.

11. Dietrich Bonhoeffer, *Life Together*, trans. Daniel W. Bloesch (Minneapolis: Fortress Press, 2015), 35.

12. Wendy Speake and Kelli Stuart, *Life Creative: Inspiration for Today's Renaissance Mom* (Grand Rapids: Kregel, 2016), 79.

13. Blanchard, Graves, and Kwan, *From Concept to Scale*, 86.

14. Ibid., 128–29.

15. The most awarded TV drama of all time, I might add.

16. To watch this great scene, visit calledtocreate.org/westwing.

17. Sally Lloyd-Jones, *The Jesus Storybook Bible: Every Story Whispers His Name* (New York: HarperCollins, 2007), 74.

Chapter 9 Renewing Our Minds

1. "Blue Pill or Red Pill—The Matrix (2/9) Movie CLIP (1999)," YouTube video, 2:40, uploaded by Movieclips, May 26, 2011, https://www.youtube.com/watch?v=zE7PKRjrid4.

2. T. C., "The Economist Explains: The Difference between Virtual and Augmented Reality," *The Economist*, April 14, 2016, http://www.economist.com/blogs/economist-explains/2016/04/economist-explains-8.

3. Ibid.

4. Marilyn Stewart, "The Inklings: A Fellowship of Imagination," *CBN*, accessed April 18, 2017, http://www1.cbn.com/inklings-fellowship-imagination.

5. Colin Duriez, *Bedeviled: Lewis, Tolkien and the Shadow of Evil* (Downers Grove, IL: InterVarsity, 2015), 65.

6. J. R. R. Tolkien, *Tales from the Perilous Realm* (New York: Houghton Mifflin Harcourt, 2012), 286.

7. Ibid., 311.

8. Ibid., 302–3.

9. Keller and Alsdorf, *Every Good Endeavor*, 29.

10. Ibid.

Chapter 10 Commanded to Create Disciples

1. "Downline Discipleship, Marching Orders: Bringing Clarity to the Commission of Christ—Part 2," Right Now Media video, posted by Kennon Vaughan, https://www.rightnow.org/Content/Series/436#2.

2. Mark L. Russell, *The Missional Entrepreneur: Principles and Practices for Business as Mission* (Birmingham, AL: New Hope Publishers, 2011), Kindle loc. 1570–77.

3. Ibid., Kindle loc. 1166–67.

4. Sebastian Traeger and Greg Gilbert, *The Gospel at Work: How Working for King Jesus Gives Purpose and Meaning to Our Jobs* (Grand Rapids: Zondervan, 2013), 126.

5. T. G. Soares, "Paul's Missionary Methods," *Biblical World* 34 (1909): 326–36, esp. 335. Cited in Ronald Hock, *The Social Context of Paul's Ministry: Tentmaking and Apostleship* (Minneapolis: Fortress Press, 1980), 88.

6. Russell, *Missional Entrepreneur*, Kindle loc. 1732–42.

7. Disclosure: I have had the privilege of working with Hardiman on a number of different projects through the years.

8. Russell, *Missional Entrepreneur*, Kindle loc. 2428–32.

9. Ibid., Kindle loc. 2537–42.

10. "Every Life Has a Story," YouTube video, posted by Dan T. Cathy, December 15, 2010, https://www.youtube.com/watch?v=2v0RhvZ3lvY.

11. To view this video, visit calledtocreate.org/cfa.

12. Cathy, *Eat Mor Chikin: Inspire More People*, 48.

13. This person's name and some other minor details of their story have been changed to conceal their identity.

Chapter 11 The Purpose of Profit

1. The White House, Office of the Press Secretary, "Remarks by the President at a Campaign Event in Roanoke, Virginia," July 13, 2012, https://www.whitehouse.gov/the-press-office/2012/07/13/remarks-president-campaign-event-roanoke-virginia.

2. Aaron Blake, "Obama's 'You Didn't Build That' Problem," *The Washington Post*, July 18, 2012, https://www.washingtonpost.com/blogs/the-fix/post/obamas-you-didnt-build-that-problem/2012/07/18/gJQAJxyotW_blog.html.

3. Greg Laurie, "Money and Motives," *OnePlace*, http://www.oneplace.com/ministries/a-new-beginning/read/articles/money-and-motives-9220.html.

4. Timothy Keller, *Preaching: Communicating Faith in an Age of Skepticism* (New York: Penguin Random House, 2015), 136.

5. "Cher Wang," *CNBC*, http://www.cnbc.com/2014/04/29/25-cher-wang.html.

6. "The World's 100 Most Powerful Women," *Forbes*, http://www.forbes.com/power-women/list/2/#tab:overall.

7. Michal Lev-Ram, "Cher Wang: A Visionary Tech Founder Returns," *Fortune*, July 7, 2014, http://fortune.com/2014/07/07/cher-wang-htc.

8. Laura M. Holson, "With Smartphones, Cher Wang Made Her Own Fortune," *The New York Times*, October 26, 2008, http://www.nytimes.com/2008/10/27/technology/companies/27wang.html.

9. Li Xin Rong, "Cher Wang, Co-founder of Mobile Giant HTC, Speaks of Her Life Testimony," *The Gospel Herald*, January 28, 2013, http://www.gospelherald.com/article/ministries/47930/cher-wang-co-founder-of-mobile-giant-htc-speaks-of-her-life-testimony.htm#.UYWEeaKG3VE.

10. "HTC Corporation," Yahoo! Finance, http://finance.yahoo.com/echarts?s=2498.TW+Interactive#{"range":"10y","allowChartStacking":true}.

11. Francis Tsai, "A Spiritual Spending Spree from Cher Wang," *Taipei Times*, February 10, 2014, http://www.taipeitimes.com/News/editorials/archives/2014/02/10/2003583151.

12. Liz Essley Whyte, "Giving It All," *Philanthropy*, Spring 2014, http://www.philanthropyroundtable.org/topic/donor_intent/giving_it_all1.

13. Ibid.

14. Ibid.

15. Ibid.

16. Bill Yenne, *Guinness: The 250 Year Quest for the Perfect Pint* (Hoboken, NJ: Wiley, 2007).

17. Patrick Lynch and John Vaizey, *Guinness's Brewery in the Irish Economy 1759–1876* (Cambridge, UK: Cambridge University Press, 2011).

18. Mansfield, "The Story of God and Guinness."

19. "Stephen Mansfield: God and Guinness," *Faith & Leadership*, August 16, 2010, https://www.faithandleadership.com/qa/stephen-mansfield-god-and-guinness.

20. Ibid.

21. Scott Snook, Brittany Raetzman, Christine Schoppe, and Jennifer Schoppe, "Bandwidth.com: Answering the Call (Case 416-014)," *Harvard Business Review*, August 2015.

22. Ibid.

23. Ibid.

24. Bill Peel, "Faith and Profit Are Not Mutually Exclusive—An Interview with Henry Kaestner," *Center for Faith & Work*, http://centerforfaithandwork.com/article/faith-and-profit-are-not-mutually-exclusive-%E2%80%94-interview-henry-kaestner.

25. Ibid.

Chapter 12 Creating for the Kingdom

1. Thiel and Wright actually joined together for two talks, both fascinating. To view them both, visit calledtocreate.org/thiel.

2. Crouch, *Culture Making*, 97.

3. "What Is the Hope for Humanity? A Discussion of Technology, Politics, and Theology," YouTube video, posted by The Veritas Forum, May 22, 2014, https://www.youtube.com/watch?v=N9Mlu7sHEHE.

4. Sean Salai, SJ, "Faith & Technology: Q&A with Peter Thiel," *America: The National Catholic Review*, October 1, 2014, http://americamagazine.org/content/all-things/faith-technology-qa-peter-thiel.

5. John Mark Comer, *Garden City: Work, Rest, and the Art of Being Human* (Grand Rapids: Zondervan, 2015), 238.

6. Alcorn, *Heaven*, xvi.

7. Apologies, Carrie Underwood.

8. Randy Alcorn, "Where God's People Go When They Die," *Eternal Perspective Ministries*, October 18, 2013, http://www.epm.org/blog/2013/Oct/18/gods-people-go.

9. N. T. Wright, *Surprised by Hope: Rethinking Heaven, the Resurrection, and the Mission of the Church* (New York: HarperCollins, 2008), 193.

10. Crouch, *Culture Making*, 107.

Want more
inspiration and
encouragement
as you follow the
CALL TO CREATE?

VISIT CALLEDTOCREATE.ORG

CONNECT WITH
Jordan!

JordanRaynor.com

JordanRaynor

LIKE THIS
BOOK?
Consider sharing it with others!

- Share or mention the book on your social media platforms. Use the hashtag **#CalledToCreate**.

- Write a book review on your blog or on a retailer site.

- Pick up a copy for friends, family, or strangers— anyone who you think would enjoy and be challenged by its message!

- Share this message on Twitter or Facebook: **I loved #CalledToCreate by @JordanRaynor // @ReadBakerBooks**

- Recommend this book for your church, workplace, book club, or class.

- Follow Baker Books on social media and tell us what you like.

 Facebook.com/ReadBakerBooks

 @ReadBakerBooks